How to Do
Everything
with

Photoshop
Elements

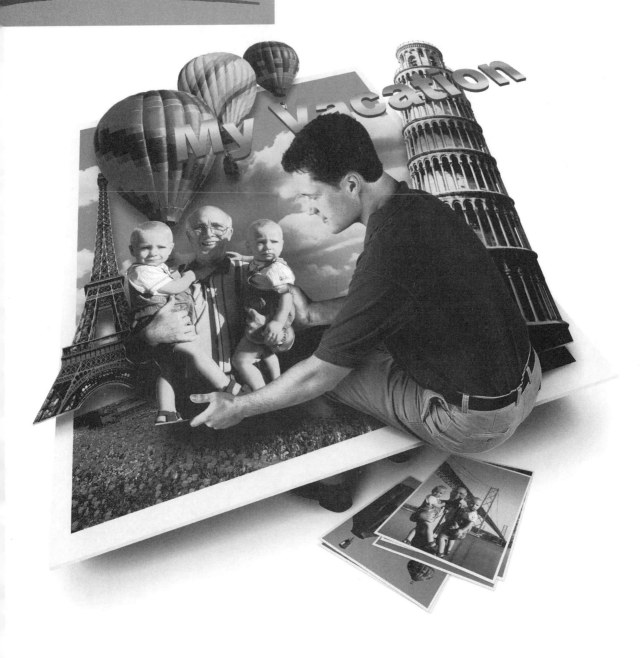

How to Do *Everything* with

Photoshop Elements

Molly Joss

Osborne/McGraw-Hill

New York Chicago San Francisco Lisbon
London Madrid Mexico City Milan New Delhi
San Juan Seoul Singapore Sydney Toronto

Osborne/**McGraw-Hill**
2600 Tenth Street
Berkeley, California 94710
U.S.A.
To arrange bulk purchase discounts for sales promotions, premiums, or fund-raisers, please contact Osborne/**McGraw-Hill** at the above address. For information on translations or book distributors outside the U.S.A., please see the International Contact Information page immediately following the index of this book.

How to Do Everything with Photoshop Elements

34567890 FGR FGR 0198765432

ISBN 0-07-219184-8

Publisher
Brandon A. Nordin

Vice President & Associate Publisher
Scott Rogers

Acquisitions Editor
Megg Bonar

Project Editor
Jennifer Malnick

Acquisitions Coordinator
Alissa Larson, Alex Corona

Technical Editor
Brian O'Neil Hughes

Copy Editor
Bob Campbell

Proofreader
Daniel Esch

Indexer
Valerie Robbins

Computer Designer
Maureen Forys,
Happenstance Type-O-Rama

Illustrator
Lyssa Wald

Series Design
Mickey Galicia

Cover Design
Dodie Shoemaker, Tom Willis, Joseph Humphrey, and Greg Scott

This book was composed with QuarkXPress 4.11 on a Macintosh G4.

Dedication

To my brothers and sisters: Jack (Bubber), Patty, Bonnie, Vickie, Trentis (Butch), Frank, and William (Bo). Thanks for being there and thanks for all the pictures!

About the Author

Molly Joss is a writer and teacher with almost 20 years' experience working with computers. For more than 15 years, one of her main focuses has been the graphic arts, including how to make bad pictures look better. She has written for more than a dozen publications, and is the author of six books—including three related to image editing. She also teaches Photoshop classes.

Contents at a Glance

Contents

Acknowledgments

For several years I have taken my own photographs for books. I get the kind of images I want and I don't have to worry about copyright issues! I want to thank the family and friends who allowed me to include my photographs of them in this book. I also want to thank my niece Amy for having such a beautiful daughter named Hope, and for allowing me to use photographs of her in the book. I also want to thank the folks who are responsible for keeping up Green Lane Park in Montgomery County, Pennsylvania, where I took the outdoor shots for the book.

Thanks too to my students for asking questions that kept me on my toes about what kinds of things people really want to know about how image editing software works and what they can do with it.

Also, special thanks to Susan Doering and Aya Taketomi at Adobe for their support of this book; and a big thank you to Brian O'Neil Hughes of Adobe for his technical editing. Finally, thank you to Lyssa Wald and the Osborne Illustration group for their hard work on the color insert.

Introduction

How Is This Book Organized?

This book is organized into three areas: getting started, getting down to business, and getting ready to communicate your images. The first few chapters introduce you to the tools in Elements and to some of the terminology and concepts used in image editing in general.

The middle section of the book is where the action is—where you learn by doing the projects outlined step-by-step. This section of the book resembles an image cookbook, so flip through these chapters, and when you see an image you like, stop and work through that project. Most of the projects are self-contained, but a few build on each other. No single project should take you more than 20 minutes to do, and most only take a few minutes.

The last few chapters of the book are devoted to helping you learn how to get your images ready for the world—by printing them, saving them, or putting them on the Web. With the information contained in these chapters you will be able to disseminate your images quickly and easily. Creating them is only part of the work you need to do—great images, like great art, need to be seen to be appreciated.

Whom Is This Book Written For?

This book is written for anyone who is interested in getting the most out of Photoshop Elements. Even the experienced graphic artist who retouches photographs in her sleep will find something interesting in this book. That said, you'll learn the most from this book if you are not a graphics guru. Let me give you some examples:

- If you don't have a lot of training when it comes to correcting image problems, you'll benefit from reading this book.

- If you don't have a lot of time to learn on your own, this book is for you. You'll be able to find what you need to know and learn how to do it in minutes.

■ If you have lots of images and some image-editing experience, you'll find ways to save time by reading this book.

■ If you want to learn how to do more with the images and photographs you have, this book will teach you many ways to do just that.

What's So Great About This Book?

This book is amazing because the author (that's me) knows you don't have a lot of time to devote to learning a program and that you really want to get down to brass tacks and get something done. So, I show you how to get stuff done—project after project, chapter after chapter. There's some theory woven into the practice, but not so much that you feel you're in a college lecture class.

This book is also great because you don't have to sit down and read it cover to cover. You can skip around, trying different projects, and learn as you go. You can read the book by itself, but the best thing to do is to sit down with the book at your computer, launch Elements, and do some of the projects. You can even skip over the first few chapters of the book if you want to get right down to business. However, I hope you will read those chapters at some point because they contain a lot of useful information.

Getting stuff done while you learn and have fun—what else do you need to make a book like this a great one?

Part I

Get Acquainted with Photoshop Elements

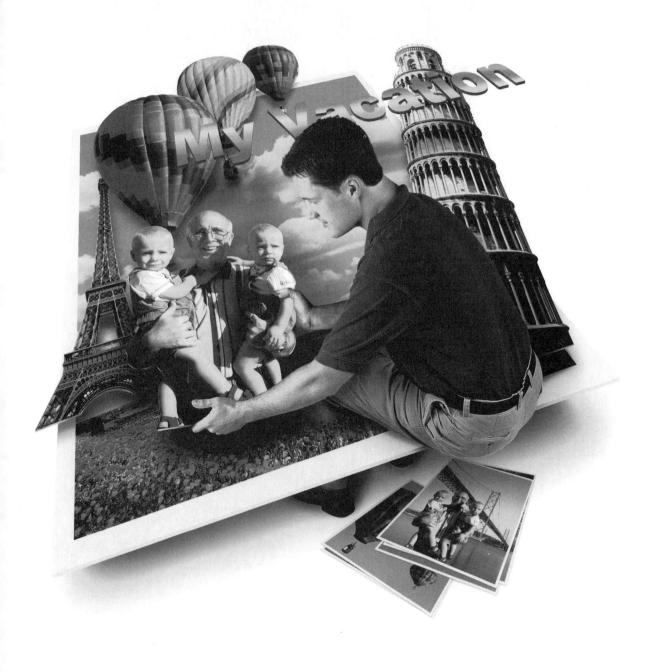

Chapter 1

Get to Know Photoshop Elements

How to...

- Understand what Photoshop Elements can do
- Navigate through the program
- Adjust your work environment

Photoshop Elements is a new, powerful, and easy-to-use program for working with images. You can use it to correct common image problems, such as red eye, but you can also use it to enhance images. Plus, you can even create your own images from scratch.

You'll be amazed to learn how easy it is to use the program—even with all that power at your disposal. Anyone can use this program and with a little practice get the most amazing results. You don't have to be a professional graphic artist—really, you don't! You can do this stuff and have fun doing it.

Working through this book will take you a long way toward becoming an Elements expert. Toss in a dash of creativity and mix well with a little experience, and soon you will be able to produce finished images that look as though an artist worked for days or weeks to create them.

In this chapter, I'll show you a few examples of the full capabilities of the program, to whet your appetite for learning and exploring. I want you to understand that Elements can do much more than correct simple image editing problems, although it is fully capable of handling those. I want you to see that you can use the program for much more than you may have imagined—and have fun in the process.

As you might imagine, though, because Elements can do so much, there is a lot to learn about the program before you actually get started. You need to learn how to navigate your way through the menus and the tools before you do anything else. You'll also need to find out how to get help when you need it. Finally, I want to show you how to customize your work environment inside Elements so that you have plenty of room to work.

I am sure you are eager to get to work, but you will find it helpful to take the time to read through this chapter. If you are comfortable and familiar with the look and feel of the program before we move on, you'll learn faster and get more done in less time.

You Can Make Simple Edits to Your Images

When you make a simple edit, you are making a change that can be done in a step or two. One example of a simple edit is to correct a problem with the entire photograph (such as the image being too dark). Another is to remove a section of an image that you don't want in the final image. Other simple edits include rotating an image or removing red eye. Most simple edits, such as the ones shown by the change from Figure 1-1 (the original) to Figure 1-2 (the edited version), take less than a minute to do in Elements once you know how to do them—and the best way to do that is to read this book (of course)!

FIGURE 1-1   This is the original image

Most images are not perfectly suited for your use, so you are going to need to edit them. Even something as simple as rotating an image or removing part of it can improve it tremendously. So, even if your image is fine the way it is, see if one or two simple edits would improve it.

FIGURE 1-2   This is the edited version; I removed part of the image and flipped what was left horizontally

You Can Make Complex Edits to Your Images

Complex edits are changes and corrections that take a little more time—a few minutes or more—and require more than a step or two to complete. Removing an irregularly shaped object from an image or removing more than one piece of an image is an example of a more complex edit. So is creating a collage using several images—or combining several simple edits to get just the right finished product.

Like simple edits, complex edits in Elements are easy to do once you know what the program can do and learn how to control the changes you're making. In other words, you have to practice making complex edits in order to learn how to make the best of the tools Elements, or any other image editing program, has to offer.

Here are a few examples of complex edits. The first image (see Figure 1-3) is the original; the second (see Figure 1-4) and third (see Figure 1-5) are edited versions of the original.

FIGURE 1-3   Here's the original image

In this first image, I deleted part of the original. I also cropped the image and made it easier to read the lettering in the sign by sharpening only that part of the image. In the third image, I applied a filter to the entire edited image.

Filters are the gateway to some of the most powerful image changing capabilities in Elements. A filter automatically changes an image in a preset way, so using even one filter can alter an image dramatically in just a few seconds. I will tell you more about filters later on in the book, and the color insert has quite a few examples of how you can use filters.

| FIGURE 1-4 | Removing part of an image zeros in on the part of the image that is most essential |

| FIGURE 1-5 | Applying a filter to an image lets you change the entire look of an image with one step |

You Can Use Filters to Modify Your Images

Elements allows you to use filters (preset special effects) to quickly change the look of an image. You can add third-party filters at any time, but so many filters come with Elements that you have plenty to work with for a while!

Applying a filter is easy and fast to do, but to get the most out of them requires learning how to adjust the controls. You also need to spend some creative time trying out different effects; there are so many of them, you owe it to yourself to try more than a few!

Here are just a few examples of the results you can create with filters inside Elements. I started with the original image and applied two different filters: the Bas Relief and the Sprayed Strokes filters.

The original image was just a set of simple shapes, really. You can see those shapes in Figure 1-6, even though I used a filter to get an embossed image (the Bas Relief filter).

Figure 1-7 shows the combination of the Bas Relief filter and the Sprayed Strokes filter. As you can see, you can apply multiple filters to change the results you'll get.

FIGURE 1-6   Here's the image with the Bas Relief filter applied to it

FIGURE 1-7   The same image with a second filter, Sprayed Strokes, now applied

You Can Add Text to Your Images

You can add simple pieces of text to images inside Elements in a few seconds. Or you can spend a little more time and add text that is truly decorative. Whatever you add to the image becomes part of the image, so once you understand the text capabilities of the program, you can use text to enhance images.

You Can Create New Images from Scratch

If your mother baked from scratch, as mine did, you can appreciate the taste difference between scratch baking and using a mix. There's nothing wrong with using a mix, but nothing beats the taste of originality you get when you mix the ingredients yourself. In Elements, you can create images from scratch by drawing or by combining elements from other images. Now, you're really cooking....

Here are two images created from scratch in Elements: In Figure 1-8, you'll see a figure that looks as though it has been sketched by hand, but all I did was draw a few simple shapes in Elements and apply a few of the artistic filters.

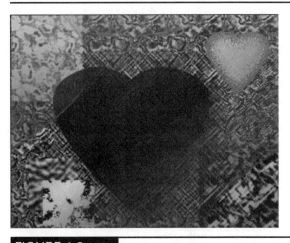

FIGURE 1-8   I drew some images using the drawing tools and applied a filter

Elements has filters that help you edit images—to remove dust and noise that may have gotten into the image. It also comes with filters that help you add an artistic look to your images. I used a few of the filters to create the image shown in Figure 1-9.

FIGURE 1-9   This object would be right at home on a sophisticated and sleek Web page; to create it, I again drew some shapes and applied some filters

Learn the Elements Interface

The user interface in Elements is the first thing you encounter when you start the program, once the opening screens have appeared. Think of the interface as scenery onstage in a theater that you get to interact with to direct the action in a play. You call the shots.

The two major components of the interface are menus and tools. Since you are familiar with other software programs, you have seen and worked with menus and tools before. So, getting accustomed to the Elements interface will be simple once you understand where all the components are, how to get them to display, and what you can change using the various components.

Use the Elements Menus to Get Your Work Done

When you start Elements for the first time, the handy QuickStart menu will appear. From here you can quickly access some of the major functions of the program, including opening and creating a file. Click Close to close this window unless you want to use one of the functions listed in it.

You can tell Elements not to show you the QuickStart menu every time you open the program (deselect the check box in the lower left of the screen), but I recommend you leave this feature enabled. The QuickStart menu lets you get a jumpstart on many of the functions of the program. By selecting one of the items on the menu, such as Open, you can bypass the menus and get right to what you want to do. Other items on the menu include acquiring an image, opening a tutorial, and pasting material from the Clipboard.

The menus in Elements are at the top of the screen underneath the title bar of the window. Through the menus, you can access all of the capabilities of the program. For example, you can print a file by clicking the printer icon on the toolbar, but you will find the actions related to printing, such as Print Preview and Page Setup, on the File menu. So, whenever you find yourself wondering where you can find something you're looking for, checking out the menus is a good starting point. You have to click a menu in order to see the drop-down segment of the menu. As in other software programs, portions of the menu that are "grayed out" are part of that menu but can't be used at the moment. Whenever you see a small triangle on a menu, you know there is another menu that branches off from there.

NOTE *The Variations submenu lets you see and choose from many versions of the same image as it would appear made lighter or darker. If you want to control how items relate to one another by grouping and ungrouping them, you can also do that via this menu.*

As you move through the book, you'll have the chance to explore each menu and its submenus in depth—believe me, we leave no menu option unexplored. So here we're going to take a quick look at each menu, and I'll tell you a few things you can do using each of the menus.

Menu	What You Can Do (Among Other Things)
File	Create new files, open existing ones
Edit	Edit images, such as by undoing or redoing changes
Image	Rotate the image, change the image size and orientation
Enhance	Make the image brighter or change the contrast
Layer	Create, select, and manipulate layers in the image
Select	Select a portion of the image for editing
Filter	Select and apply a filter
View	Zoom in, zoom out, and add a ruler around the image
Window	Show or hide windows used in the program
Help	Get instructions on how to do a particular task

NOTE

At the bottom of the Edit menu, the Preferences submenu lets you change many of the program's preset functions and controls, such as the amount of memory used by the program. If you routinely work with large files (more than a few megabytes), you might want to give Elements more RAM to work in—that will make the program run faster. See Chapter 2 for more details on this. The Preferences submenu is a short menu, but it packs some powerful capabilities into this small space!

Use Tools to Speed Up Your Edits

When you work on your house, you need a good set of tools for the job, and that set of tools can vary. When you paint, you need paintbrushes—but you also need tape and maybe some materials to help fix a few holes in the wall. When you put up wallpaper, you need a whole different set of tools.

When you edit images, you also need a wide variety of tools that were specifically designed with specific purposes in mind. You get all the tools you need in Elements to do just about anything to an image. And you never have to worry about losing one!

In Elements, the tools that you need to edit, change, and select portions of an image are located on the toolbox that appears on the left-hand side of the screen when you first start the program (see Figure 1-10). You can hide this toolbox using the Window | Hide Tools command if you want to give yourself more room while you are working, or you can move it to another part of the window. If you close the window, though, you won't have ready access to many of the tools of the program, as only a few of the tool icons are available through the Shortcuts bar underneath the Menu bar.

Keep your tools handy by leaving the toolbox open and ready to use. Look closely at the icons on the toolbox and you will see a small triangle at the bottom right-hand corner of some of them. Just as the small triangle on a menu means there is a submenu, a small triangle on a tool icon means something more is available. Click the small triangle on the icon and the icon bar above the toolbar changes (see Figure 1-11), showing you the different controls and options for that tool.

Notice, too, that when you rest the cursor over a tool icon, the name of the tool appears. This is the tool tip. You can select a tool either by clicking it or by resting the cursor on it and typing in the letter that appears in parentheses at the end of the tool tip. Look at Figure 1-12 to get more information about the tools.

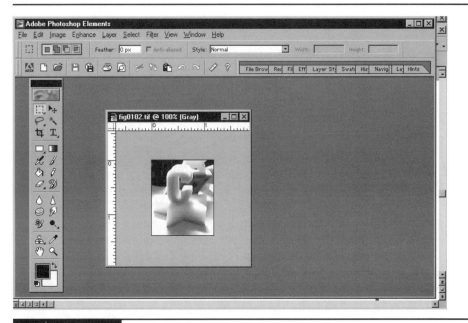

FIGURE 1-10   The toolbox automatically appears on the left side of the screen, but you can move it

FIGURE 1-11   When you click the triangle for a tool, notice that the controls for that tool change

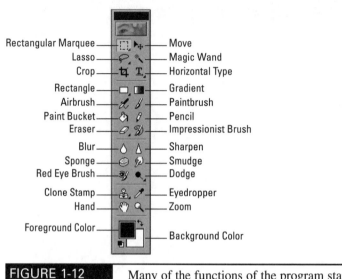

Rectangular Marquee	Move
Lasso	Magic Wand
Crop	Horizontal Type
Rectangle	Gradient
Airbrush	Paintbrush
Paint Bucket	Pencil
Eraser	Impressionist Brush
Blur	Sharpen
Sponge	Smudge
Red Eye Brush	Dodge
Clone Stamp	Eyedropper
Hand	Zoom
Foreground Color	Background Color

FIGURE 1-12   Many of the functions of the program start right here, in the Elements toolbar

Adobe also gives you a wonderfully quick way to find out more about a tool—it is the Hints palette. I tell you all about palettes later on in this chapter, but since we are talking about tools now, it makes sense for me to mention the Hints palette now. You can access it as you would any other palette, or you can select Show Hints from the Window menu.

When the Hints palette is open and you rest your cursor on a tool icon, information about the tool and how to use it shows up automatically in the Palette window. If you want to read more about a tool, using the Hints palette is faster than looking up the tool name in the Help file.

Now, let's move on to a little more detail about some of the tools. When you use one of the selection tools, such as the Rectangular Marquee or Lasso tool, you can see the area you've selected because a scrolling marquee appears around the selected area (as shown in Figure 1-13). The scrolling marquee is a moving line, much like the marquee lights that theaters used to use around their outdoor signs.

You can use the drawing or painting tools to draw shapes or to add details to an image. In Figure 1-14, I'm using the Airbrush tool to add some detail to an image. First I applied a filter, and now I am brushing out some of the edges of the image.

1

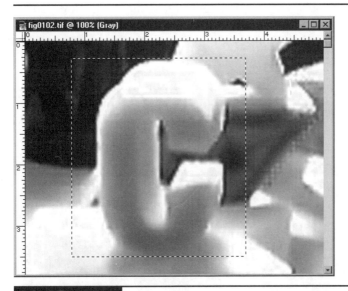

| FIGURE 1-13 | This is an example of the rectangular marquee |

| FIGURE 1-14 | I use the Airbrush tool to smooth out the edges of the larger star |

The image correction tools, such as the Sponge and Blur tools, allow you to make minor corrections to images. Sometimes we all need to fudge a bit, yes? These tools allow you to do just that. Here in Figure 1-15, I've used the Blur and Sponge tools on a portion of the background of an image.

FIGURE 1-15   The Sponge tool allows me to blur sections of the background in this image

Shortcuts and Options

Take a moment and look under the menu bar; you will see two other horizontal bars. Unlike the menus, many of which have flyout menus that appear when you click the word on the menu, the bars are arranged horizontally and do something immediately after you click an icon.

One of these bars is called the Shortcuts bar (see Figure 1-16) because you can click the icons to quickly access some of the functions of the program. If you rest your cursor on an icon, the name of the action or function appears.

FIGURE 1-16   You can quickly get to some of the program's functions from the Shortcuts bar

The other bar I want to point out to you is the Options bar (see Figure 1-17). When you click a tool, the controls for that particular tool appear on the Options bar for that tool. Click a different tool and a different set of options appears in the same place. Try that a few times so that you can see what I mean. When you are working in Elements, it's a good idea to keep an eye on the Options bar because you'll use it to access the different controls and options for a tool when you click the icon for that tool.

NOTE   *If you have used Photoshop LE, the Options bar is a new feature for you. It's a great way to access controls that are not as readily accessible in other programs.*

FIGURE 1-17   The Toolbar shows the controls for the tool you have selected

Notice that you can hide either or both of these bars, which I will show you how to do later on in this chapter. Later, when you ask Elements to show these bars again, the bar that you asked to see first slides down and the new one is shown above the first one. Thus, you could set up the interface to make the Options bar appear right under the menu bar and put the Shortcuts bar beneath the Options.

I'm pointing this out to you because the two bars change position when you hide and reveal them again later. So, if it looks as if they are moving around on you, they really are! Don't worry about it, but if you want the interface to be the same all the time, you may have to drag one of the bars from time to time.

If you find the changing order confusing, you can restore the arrangement of the two by selecting Reset Palette Locations from the Window menu.

Use Element's Palettes to Access Commonly Used Functions

If you have worked with other Adobe programs, you may be familiar with the concept of tool palettes. If not, it is not important—palettes are similar to toolboxes in that both are easy ways to get to program functions. Palettes, though, don't use icons. Instead, they use text or images to convey information.

NOTE *The palette well, located on the right-hand side of the Shortcuts bar, is where the palettes are located. You can also access the palettes by using the Show/Hide [Palette] commands on the Window menu.*

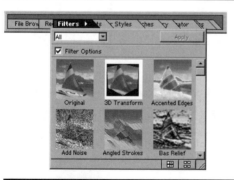

FIGURE 1-18   When you open a palette, it appears right below the well

When all the palettes are in the well, it is hard to see all of the palette names at once, so here is a list of them, plus a brief description of the function of each:

Palette	What You Can Do with It
File Browser	Quickly locate a file
Recipes	Access wizards for many different kinds of image edits
Effects	Gain quick access to many different special effects for images and text
Layer Styles	Find different effects you can apply to a layer
Swatches	Quickly pick different foreground and background colors
Filters (called Filters Browser on Window menu)	See examples of various filters
History	See the edits and changes you have made to the image
Navigator	Zoom in or out
Info	Get instant positioning feedback as you use a tool
Layers	See a list of the layers in the image (as with Info, it doesn't default to the well)
Hints	When you click a tool or palette, get information on that item (also doesn't default to the well)

You can remove a palette from the well by clicking the tab for the palette and dragging the palette elsewhere in the window. You might want to do this if you want to put that palette closer to the section of the image you are editing. To return the palette to the well, simply close it.

Look carefully at the upper right-hand corner of a palette. If a circle with a triangle is shown there, a Palette menu is associated with that palette. Click the circle/triangle to bring up the menu.

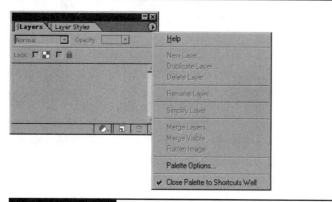

FIGURE 1-19   This is the Palette menu for the Layers palette, which appears after you click on the circle/triangle

When You Need Help

Even with a resource like this one to help you, it is hard to remember what everything in Elements is or why it is there. When you're looking for a quick refresher or you want to get some quick information about a tool, don't forget to check the Help files. You can also look in the Help files for instructions on how to carry out all of the image edits and changes in Elements.

To access the help files, select Help | Help Contents and search for the information you need. You can also click the question mark on the Shortcuts bar to open up the Help files.

In addition, all the palettes and other areas of the program have Help buttons on their boxes. If you see a Help button on a box, clicking it will take you directly to that portion of the Help files. There is also the Hints palette, which gives you a short, to-the-point description of the program's functions and links you directly to the Help files for each function.

Maximize Your Work Area

When you start Elements, several menu bars appear, as well as the toolbox. As you open a file and start using the program, you may find that you need to see more of the image you want to edit. In fact, that will be the case most of the time. So, let me show you how to maximize your work area.

Hide the Options bar by selecting Window | Hide Options. Use Window | Hide Shortcuts to hide the Shortcuts bar. Now that you have more room, you can decide to hide the toolbox or to simply move it aside. Now you have plenty of room to work.

 You can also hide the toolbox by selecting Window | Hide Tools; or you can just press TAB.

Chapter 2

Prepare to Use Photoshop Elements

How to...

- Get ready to use the software
- Adjust your monitor settings for better images
- Reduce eyestrain
- Improve the performance of your computer

Why You Need to Prepare

Elements is all about images—not text-only documents, as is the case with office-related computer software. To get the most out of your time with Elements, you need to adjust your computer and monitor to handle and display images properly.

The changes you make in this chapter won't adversely affect the other work you do with your computer but will help you get the most productivity out of your work inside Elements.

Eliminate Unnecessary Hurdles to Getting Good Color

Just as you take the time to adjust the color on your television the first time you use it and periodically thereafter to get the best picture, you need to adjust your computer monitor when you work with imageediting software. If you adjust your monitor, you will be able to make changes to the color in images that will help you get the most accurate color when you print the images. In this chapter, I will show you how to make those changes.

Reduce Eyestrain

Staring at your computer screen all day can give you headaches and make your eyes hurt. So, let me encourage you to treat yourself gently and take breaks on a frequent basis. Turn your attention, and your eyes, to something other than the screen for a few minutes as often as you can. Even a few minutes out of every 30 spent looking out the window or reading something on paper can help.

Another thing that helps reduce eyestrain and headaches is adjusting your monitor properly. You will adjust the brightness and contrast later in this chapter when you use the Adobe Gamma software, but there are other settings on your monitor that you should adjust.

These settings vary with different monitors, so check the owner's manual that came with the monitor for information on the settings and how to change them.

Adjust Your Monitor to Get More Accurate Colors

When you change a monitor to more accurately display the true colors in an image, you are calibrating it. You need to calibrate your monitor before you start using Elements, and you need to recalibrate it periodically. Once a month is a good schedule if you use the monitor less than a few days a week. If you use it every day, try to calibrate it once every week to ten days or at least before the next time you use Elements.

Fortunately, Adobe provides a calibration utility called Adobe Gamma with each copy of Elements. Adobe Gamma installs itself on your computer when you install Elements. There are other ways of calibrating your monitor, such as other software packages. There are even small hardware devices that attach to the screen and read the amount of light coming from the screen. You don't need to invest in these kinds of tools unless you want to be a professional designer or graphic artist. Using Adobe Gamma on a regular basis is all you need to calibrate your monitor.

That said, here are some helpful hints that I'd like to pass along to you. You won't need software or hardware to do these. Just a little common sense and a little window cleaner and a soft cloth will do. You may need to move your monitor so that light from a window or a lighting fixture is not falling on the screen. Turn the monitor away from any direct source of light.

Next, clean the screen on a regular basis. Glasses get smudged and dirty, and so do computer screens. Use an ordinary window cleaner and that soft cloth I mentioned to clean the monitor (or screen). Never spray the cleaner directly onto the glass, as you might accidentally spray the control buttons on the monitor as well. Spray the cleaner onto the cloth and wipe the screen gently to remove dust and smudges.

How to ...

Make Sure Your PC Monitor Is Set for Maximum Color Display

Before you use the Adobe Gamma utility (see the next section), take a few minutes to make sure your monitor is set to display the maximum number of colors it is able to show. Click Start and select Settings from the list that appears. Select Control Panel from the list and the Control Panel window opens. Double-click the Display icon; the Display Properties dialog box opens. Click the Settings tab. Make sure the Colors setting (left-hand side of the window) is set at the highest possible color setting. On newer monitors, this is True Color (24 bit). To change the setting, click the down arrow next to the current choice to bring up the list of settings. Click the one you want to select it. Click OK to close the window and instigate the change.

Did you know?

Whenever you see an Apply button in an Elements dialog box, you can click that button to apply a change and then continue to make more changes. If you want to make more than one change, remember to click Apply after every change and then click OK when you are finished making all your changes. If you have just one change to make, though, you can skip clicking Apply and just click OK.

Find and Start Using the Adobe Gamma Utility

Before you run the Gamma program, make sure your monitor has had a chance to warm up—make sure it's been on for at least half an hour. To find and initiate the Gamma program:

1. If you have a Windows computer, from the Start button, select Settings | Control Panel. You will see the icon for the Adobe Gamma program on the

Control Panel window, as shown in the following illustration. If you have a Macintosh, from the Apple menu, select Control Panels | Adobe Gamma. The Adobe Gamma icon looks a lot like the Display icon, so look for the label beneath the icon to find the correct one.

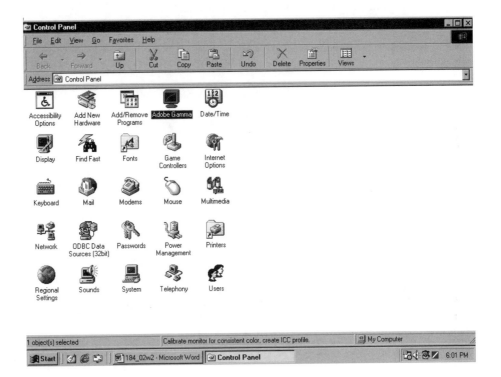

2. Double-click the Adobe Gamma icon to start the process.

Use the Step-by-Step Wizard

Unless you've had experience creating color profiles for computer monitors before, you should use the Step-by-Step Wizard in the Gamma program. It will guide you through the process of calibrating your monitor.

Here's how to use the wizard:

1. Make sure the Step-by-Step Wizard is selected on the opening screen. Click Next to continue.

2. A monitor profile name will appear in the box on the next window. Select another profile only if you know the one shown is incorrect; otherwise, let the program pick the profile. Click Next to continue.

3. Following the instructions on the screen, adjust the brightness and contrast on your monitor. Click Next to continue.

Shown next is what an image in Elements could look like if you have the brightness and contrast set too low:

Here's the same image with the brightness and contrast set correctly:

2

4. The software will display the manufacturer's name or the type of phosphors used in your monitor. Unless you know this information is incorrect, do not change the program's selection. Click Next to continue.

5. Use the slider to adjust the single gamma until the edges of the box fade slightly.

   In the next illustration, I have adjusted the gamma until the edges of the box are readily visible. This isn't what you want. You want to adjust the gamma until you barely see the edges of the box, and keep adjusting the gamma until you can't really distinguish the edges of the box.

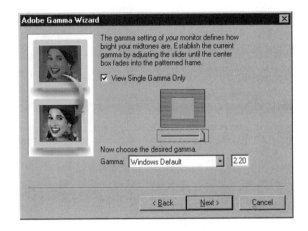

NOTE   *Leave the default gamma settings for your monitor as the program has them set up.*

6. Click Next to continue.

7. The white point of your monitor is shown next, and Adobe Gamma has estimated the correct setting. Leave this setting unless you want to spend some time following the steps for measuring the white point. If you want to do that, click Measure and follow the instructions. When you are done, or to leave the setting, click Next to continue.

8. Leave the adjusted white point the same as the Hardware setting. Click Next to continue.

9. Click Before to see the monitor as it displayed images before you made changes. Click After to see the changes you've made. The differences may be subtle. Click Finish to save your changes.

Give your new, modified monitor profile its own name by changing the name of the profile before you save it.

Saving the new settings with a different name leaves the original profile intact in case you later change monitors and need to use the profile again (see Figure 2-1).

Do not use the original name when you save your edited profile

Speed Up Your Computer So That Images Redraw Faster

Since a computer has to gather up all the image data before it can show you an image onscreen, the faster your computer is, the faster you will be able to see the image. The same is true for the speed at which you can see changes you've made to images. In general, the larger the file size of an image or the more complicated it is, the slower it is to show up (to be rendered) on screen.

In the pre-Pentium days, rendering speeds used to be frustratingly slow, and you could literally sit in front of your screen for minutes waiting for a large image to render completely. Today, with faster-than-ever computers, this has changed, although you may find when you're working with a large image that the rendering time is slower than you would like.

So, I'm going to explain a few ways to increase the rendering speed of your computer so that you cut waiting time down to the lowest possible amount of time.

Enable Pixel Doubling

Inside of Elements you can change the default Preference's settings for many different aspects of using the software, including some settings that affect how the display functions. One of these display-related preferences is pixel doubling—a way Adobe has developed for speeding up the display of images inside Elements.

When pixel doubling is enabled, the size of the individual pixels in the image preview is temporarily doubled. The size of the pixels in the image is not affected in any way. So, before you start using Elements, it's a good idea to turn pixel doubling on. It only takes a few steps to do this, and here's how you do it:

1. Select Preferences from the Edit menu.

2. Choose Display & Cursors from the Preferences menu.

3. Click the box next to Use Pixel Doubling.

4. Click OK to save the choice and close the window.

Increase the Amount of RAM Photoshop Elements Can Use

Each software program on your computer needs to use part of the random access memory (RAM) installed on your computer. The operating system dips into this shared resource when you turn the computer on. When you start using a program, it grabs a portion of the remaining amount of memory to use as its workspace while you are using the program. When you stop using the program, the application releases its hold on the RAM, freeing it up for use by other programs.

Now that I've told you this, it is just a quick, intuitive jump in thinking to realize that the more memory a program has, the faster it can get its work done. Yes and no— yes if the program could use the elbow room the extra memory gives it and no if the program can do the work just fine using the default amount of memory.

With Elements, the answer is a definite yes—especially if you are working with large and complex files or if you routinely use filters to alter images. So, I recommend giving Elements a generous slice of your computer's RAM, more than it takes for itself by default. It's easy to do this, and it only requires a few steps:

1. Select Preferences from the Edit menu.

2. Select Memory & Image Cache from the Preferences menu.

3. As you can see in the following illustration, the total amount of memory available for use by Elements is listed, as is the percentage the program is

currently using. The default is 50%. Type in **70%**. The new RAM setting will not be used until you exit and reenter the program.

4.   Click OK to save the new setting and close the window.

Other Changes to Make in Elements

You may find that, after making all the changes I have suggested in the earlier sections of this chapter, you are happy with how quickly Elements runs on your computer. If you are not and you find that, once you start working with Elements, the program is slower than you would like, come back to this section. Try the suggestions I've made here if you want to make sure your computer is operating at peak capacity.

The recommendations I make here are not as easy or as simple to put into practice as the others in this chapter. That's why I suggest that you make the changes I have outlined earlier and then make these only if you are still dissatisfied with the speed of Elements.

Add RAM to Your Computer

Image editing programs like to have a lot of memory at their disposal—they like to have a lot of elbow room while they are working. When you bought your computer, you may not have thought about purchasing extra RAM because you may not have known you were going to use your computer to edit images. So, you may need to increase the amount of RAM on your computer. After you do so, make sure you have given Elements permission to use a higher percentage of the available RAM, as I have outlined earlier in the chapter.

Adobe suggests you have a minimum of 64 megabytes of RAM installed on your computer to use Elements. If you do not have that amount of memory on your computer, you should definitely add enough to get to that level. If you don't have it, you may find that larger files take a long time to render or that Elements doesn't have enough system resources to complete an operation.

People always ask if you should have more than the minimum amount of RAM. I have talked to a lot of professional graphic artists, and they always say they add as much memory to their computers as they can. If you can afford it and want to use Elements a lot, I suggest you do the same; 128 megabytes is a good amount of RAM to start with.

If you use a Macintosh computer, please check to make sure that the Virtual Memory setting is enabled.

Did you know?

When you work on the PC, an application can save files temporarily on your hard disk, and you can delete those temporary files later to free up disk space. Search for all files with the .tmp extension and delete the files you find. The operating system may not let you delete some files because those files are needed by the computer for work in progress. That's okay—just delete the files the computer will allow you to remove. You may end up with megabytes of recovered disk space!

Free Up Space on Your Hard Drive

When Elements does not have enough RAM to complete an operation, it uses part of your computer's hard disk as if it were memory—almost as if it were virtual RAM. This capability (called scratch disk) is a great feature of the program that originated from the days when RAM was really expensive—more expensive than hard disks. It is something that happens without your being aware of it or needing to manage it.

It is also a great boon if you have added the maximum amount of memory to your computer or cannot afford to add more. Add the memory if you can, but if you can't, you will have to rely on the scratch disks to boost the program's performance.

The only catch is that Elements can only create a scratch disk out of the large chunks of available space on the hard disk. It will not delete anything that is already there or fit itself into small spaces. It looks for a large section of free space on the hard disk to use. So, to make the most of this feature, you need to make sure you have large blocks of free space available. You do that by removing unused files and by defragmenting the hard disk from time to time. You can also use a variety of disk utilities that are located in the System Tools folder on your PC. For the Macintosh, consider rebuilding your desktop. Check the Help files that come with your computer to find out how to do these routine maintenance tasks.

By the way, Adobe recommends that you have at least 130 megabytes of hard disk space available when you install Elements. As with RAM, though, most designers prefer to have double or triple the recommended amount. Since most new computers come with gigabyte hard disks, you are safe if you have not loaded the hard disk up with a lot of applications.

How to ... Set Up More than One Scratch Disk

Remember that I said Elements can use part of your hard disk as a scratch disk and that can improve the speed of your work? You don't have to set that when you install the program; Elements automatically sets it up and designates the startup hard disk as the place where it will create a scratch disk.

If your computer can access more than one hard disk, you can go one better by telling Elements which disks to use as scratch disks. Elements will use the startup disk first, then move on to the others and set up scratch disks on them. Each disk that you designate must be a separate hard disk and should not be the disk you have the program installed on, for best performance overall.

To set up additional scratch disk designations, select Preferences from the Edit menu and then pick Plug Ins & Scratch Disks from the Preferences menu. Change the first scratch disk to one other than the startup disk by clicking the down arrow and selecting another disk from the pop-up list. Select the locations for the other three scratch disks if you have enough hard disks to use. To do so, click the down arrow next to that scratch disk and select the disk from the pop-up list. Click OK to save the settings and close the window.

Summary

In this chapter, I asked you to take a little time to prepare your computer to work with Elements, and I showed you a few ways to do that. I promise you the prep time will be well worth it in return on investment—you'll have more productive work sessions and fewer frustrations.

Chapter 3

Open, Find, and Organize Your Images

How to...

- Get your picture from your scanner or digital camera into Photoshop Elements
- Open image files
- Change file size, resolution, and other image characteristics automatically
- Open files when you can't remember their exact name or location
- Organize your digital image collections

Scanners and digital cameras are great tools for capturing images. I like to think of them as the digital grist, the source material that is so imperative for the creative mind mill to function at peak capacity. In this chapter, I will tell you how to get images from either your digital camera or your scanner to Photoshop Elements, how to speed up the digital image harvest, and how to open and find images. Finally, I will tell you about contact sheets and other ways to organize your digital images.

Open an Image Using a Scanner or Digital Camera

Before you can use images from your camera or scanner in Elements, you need to do a little prep work—such as installing the software that comes with either device on the same computer as Elements. Once you have installed the software and hooked the computer up to the device via the appropriate cable, here is how to access the images:

1. Choose Import from the File menu.

2. Choose your scanner or digital camera from the menu of devices that appears.

3. The software that runs your device will automatically launch, and a preview of the image on the scanner or a gallery of the images on your digital camera will appear. Operate the scanner to get your image into Elements or select the image you want from the digital camera gallery, and the image will open as a file in Elements.

You can also start the image acquisition process by selecting Acquire from the Elements QuickStart menu that appears when you start the program. You can bring up the QuickStart menu at any point by selecting Show QuickStart from the Window menu.

Retrieve More than One Image at One Time

You can get more than one image at a time from your digital camera if your camera lets you view a gallery of images stored inside the camera. Even if your camera manual does not tell you how to do this, you may be able to do it by following this procedure:

1. Open the image gallery using the software that comes with your camera and find the files you want to retrieve.

2. Click the preview of the first image in the series. Then, hold down the CTRL key and click each of the thumbnails of the other images you want to retrieve. If you are using a Macintosh, press SHIFT, hold it down, and click on the thumbnails.

3. Click OK to retrieve the images.

Import Images from a PDF File

You can open a PDF file using the same procedure that you use to open any file, but if you only want an image from a PDF file, you need to import the image. This feature would come in handy if, for example, your company had prepared a number of documents in PDF format and you wanted to take one of the images in that document and work on it in Elements. By importing just the image, you save the time it would take to open the PDF file and cut and paste the image. Here is how you import a PDF image:

1. Select Import from the File menu.

2. Select PDF Image from the menu of file types and devices that appears.

3. When the PDF Image Import box opens, you will be able to tell how many images are in the PDF file by looking at the image count at the bottom of the window.

   When you see the image you want in the preview section of the PDF Image Import box, click OK, as shown in the next illustration.

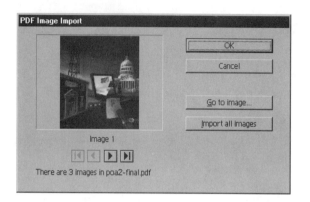

5. If the image shown is not the one you want, use the direction buttons to find the image you want to import. If you know which image you want (by the order in which it appears in the PDF document), click Go to Image and type in the number of the image.

6. If you want to import all the images in the PDF, click Import All Images.

7. Find and click the image you want to import to select it.

When Elements imports each image from a PDF file, it will create a separate file for each imported image, as shown in the following illustration:

8. If you only want one image and you see it in the preview window, click OK to import the image. Elements will import it.

9. When Elements finishes the import process, it closes the PDF file.

Did you know?

Portable Document Format (PDF) files are created in an Adobe program called Acrobat and are used to distribute documents without losing any of the formatting. There is another kind of file, called PDP (also known as Photoshop PDF), that works the same way as PDF except that you don't need the Acrobat reader to open PDP files as long as you have Photoshop or Elements installed on your computer.

Use Batch Controls to Speed Up Your Work

A batch of images is not the same as a batch of cookies—how I wish! Around lunchtime during a busy workday, I sometimes find myself wishing this were true. But the only thing the two terms have in common is that both refer to a set of items. In Elements, you can use the batch concept to speed up your image importing and some of your image editing tasks. If only it could turn out a few oatmeal raisin cookies in the same process....

Get Ready to Make the Batch

Before you make a batch of cookies, you have to gather up your ingredients. Well, you have to get ready to make an image batch in Elements by placing all the images you want to process in the batch in the same folder or in the same location on your hard disk or server.

This is easy enough to do if you are transferring digital image files or even operating the scanner from inside Elements. All it takes is a few moments to decide where the best place to keep the images is and make a destination folder. Then, as you are working, you can put the images in that new folder and leave them there until you are ready to make your batch.

You can use the batch process to change several image attributes automatically, including file type, image size, resolution, and even the name of the file.

Before you start the batch process, make sure you have enough room on your hard disk or server—wherever you want Elements to put the converted files—to accommodate the new files. If you run out of room before all the images are converted, the process will stop. You will have to make some room, make a batch out of the unconverted files, and start the batch process using those files.

Change Image Attributes Automatically

Once you are ready for the batch process, here is how to set the controls and get the process started:

1. Choose Automate from the File menu.

2. Select Batch from the menu that appears; the Batch dialog box appears.

3. Tell Elements where to find the files you want processed by clicking Source.

4. If you want to select a file type that all the converted images will have, select the file type from the drop-down list in the Conversion Options section.

5. If you want to make all the images have the same dimensions and resolution, set those specifications by entering the information in the Image Size section. You can change a lot about an image at one time, including its size and image type (see the following illustration).

6. If you want to have Elements automatically assign a new name to each file, select the Rename Files check box. Then choose the first and second parts of the new name by selecting the components from the two pop-up lists in the File Naming section.

Elements allows you to create a one- or two-part name for the new image. For the first part, you could use the document name, and for the second, the date the file was created.

Batch	☒
Files to convert: Folder ▾	OK
Source... C:\My Documents\PHLE book	Cancel
☐ Include All Subfolders	Help

Conversion Options
Convert file type: TIFF

Document Name
document name
DOCUMENT NAME
1 Digit Serial Number
2 Digit Serial Number
3 Digit Serial Number
Serial Letter (a, b, C...)
Serial Letter (A, B, C...)
mmddyy (date)
mmdd (date)
yyyymmdd (date)
yymmdd (date)
yyddmm (date)
ddmmyy (date)
ddmm (date)
extension
EXTENSION
None

Image Size
☑ Convert Image Size
Width (pixels) 300
Resolution: 150 dpi ▾

File Naming
☑ Rename Files
Example: MyFile.gif
Document Name ▾ + ▾
Compatibility: ☑ Windows ☐ Mac OS ☐ Unix

Output Options
Destination... C:\My Documents\PHLE book

TIP *Make sure to select at least one segment of the new filename that is unique to each image, such as the original filename. Otherwise, all of your new files will have identical names and overwrite each other—up to the last image—during the conversion process.*

7. If you want to change the file compatibility type from one platform to another, check the type you want by checking one of the boxes at the bottom of the File Naming section.

8. Tell Elements where to store the converted files by clicking Destination.

9. Click OK to close the window and start the process.

TIP *If you have more than a few images to process, the batch conversion process can take a few minutes or more to get the job done.*

Make and Open Image Files in Seconds

Great stars might be born and not made, but rarely do you get an image that could not stand a little improvement. In Elements, that means you have to create a new file or open an existing one before you can start the improvement campaign. In this section, I will show you how to make, open, and import files of all kinds.

Create a New File

If you are not opening an existing file, you need to create a new one from scratch. Here's how you create a new file in Elements.

1. Choose New from the Elements File menu. You can also create a new file by clicking the New button on the Shortcuts bar.

2. Give your file a name by typing it in the box in the New window that appears, which is shown in Figure 3-1. If you want to create a color image, choose RGB Color from the Mode pop-up list.

3. Enter the desired width, height, and resolution in the boxes.

4. Unless you need to have a white or solid color background, leave the Contents selection set to Transparent.

5. Click OK to create the file and close the window.

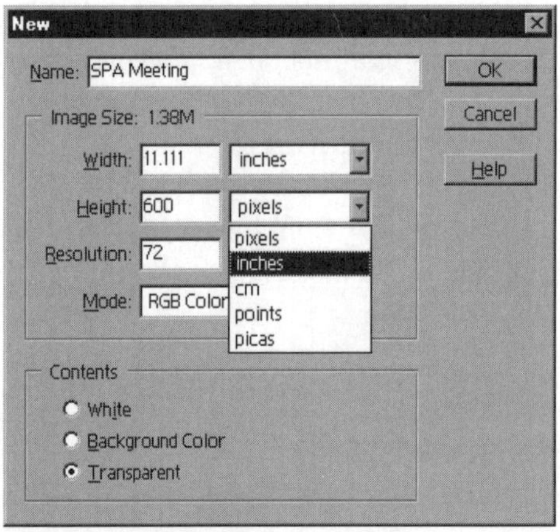

FIGURE 3-1 You can change the resolution from pixels to inches by clicking the down arrow next to the unit boxes for the width and height

Open an Existing Image File

1. Select Open from the File menu inside Elements; the Open window appears. You can also select Open from the Shortcuts bar. You can also click the Open button on the Shortcuts bar.

2. Choose the file from the list that appears in the window. If the file you want is not listed, you can use the icons at the top right of the window to locate the file.

3. Double-click the name of the file once you have found the file. Or, you can click the file once to select it and click Open.

If you haven't selected All Formats from the Files of Type dialog box, you may not see the file you are looking for. If you see that another file type is selected, click the down arrow next to this box and go to the bottom of the list where All Formats is located (see Figure 3-2).

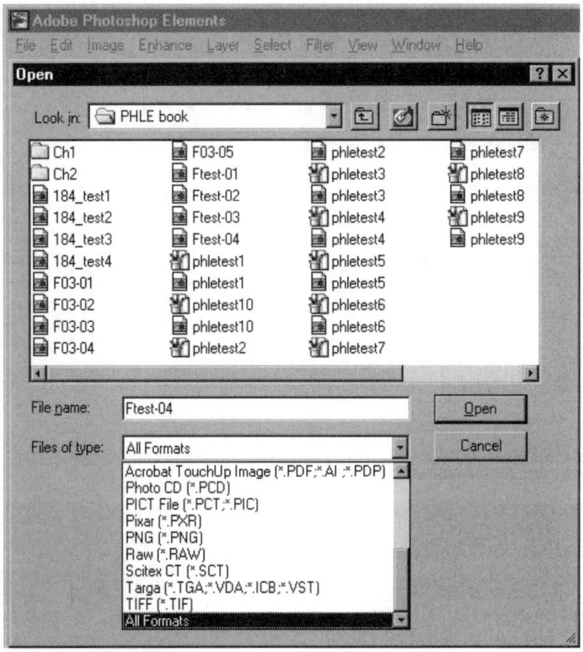

FIGURE 3-2   Make sure the Files of Type setting at the bottom of the window is set to All Formats

Open a File from the Clipboard

When you are working with a PC, whenever you copy a file or create a print of the screen by hitting the PRINT SCREEN button on your keyboard, the data is copied to the Clipboard. The Clipboard is nothing more than a portion of the computer's memory set aside for temporary storage of such items, but it is a pretty handy feature to know about when you want to copy an image and use it in another image.

Inside Elements, you can create a new file directly from the Clipboard once information has been stored on the Clipboard. Here's how you create that new file:

1. Create your Clipboard contents by copying an image or taking a shot of the screen.

2. Select From Clipboard from the File menu.

3. Elements opens a new file with the image on the Clipboard.

How to ... View the Contents of the Clipboard

You can look at the contents of the Clipboard without having to paste it into a file. To see the contents of the Clipboard, from the Start button, select Programs and then Accessories. Point to System Tools and then select Clipboard Viewer. A window will open, and you can see what's on the Clipboard.

Did you know?

The Clipboard can only hold one image at a time. After you copy an image, you have to paste it somewhere or save the Clipboard contents to a file before you can copy anything else.

When You Can't Open a File

You can use the method described here to open a file if you have tried to open the file using the method described previously and Elements cannot automatically determine the file type. Despite all of the computer industry's continuing efforts to use standard image file formats across computer platforms, there can still be some problems.

You'll know you have a file type translation problem in Elements if you try to open what you know to be a perfectly good image file only to get an error message that says the file type is not recognized. If that happens and you know what the file type is, try this:

1. Select Open As from the File menu in Elements; the Open As window appears.

2. Open the pop-up list of files in the Open As box by clicking the down arrow next to the box. Select the file format that your file is from the list.

3. Next, look at the list of filenames in the window and click the name of the file to select it. If you do not see the name of the file you want to open on the list, use the icons at the top right of the window to help locate it.

4. Double-click the filename to open the file or click it once to select it and click Open.

How to ...   Guess a File Format When You Are Not Sure What It Is

If you try to open a file in Elements using the File | Open procedure and Elements says it can't open the file because it doesn't recognize the file type, read the error message carefully. Elements will give the filename and file type (TIF, BMP, etc.) in the error message. Write the file extension down and use the File | Open As procedure outlined here. When you get to the part of the box where you select the file type, if you see the extension listed, go ahead and select that extension. Make sure to scroll through the whole list so that you don't accidentally miss it. If the file extension you are looking for isn't listed, Elements can't open that kind of file.

Find and Open an Image When You're Not Sure Where It Is

Sometimes when you are working with images, it can be difficult to find a particular file. You have forgotten either where it is or what it is called. Don't worry—this happens to everyone once in a while. Fortunately, Elements has a handy capability called the File Browser to help you find images when you are having trouble with the details. Here's how to use the File Browser:

1. Select Show File Browser from the Window menu.

2. You'll see a gallery of images in the palette area. If you do not see your image, use the drop-down list to access different areas of your hard disk or network until you see the image you want.

   If you don't immediately see your image, but you know it is in the directory shown at the top of the window, scroll through the images until you find the one you are looking for, as shown in the following illustration:

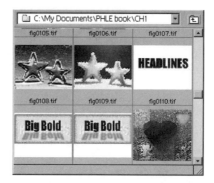

3. Double-click the image to open it. You can also click the image and drag it into the work area to open it. Or, click the image you want once and press ENTER.

SHORTCUT   *If you have worked on a file recently, use File | Open Recent to display a list of the files you have opened most recently. If the file you are looking for is listed there, click the filename to open the file. It's a handy shortcut.*

Close a File

I will tell you how to save your files later on in the book, once you have had a chance to edit some images. That is because I want to spend some time telling you what file formats are best to use and when. Making that decision depends upon what you want to do with your files after you have edited them.

You can close a file without making or saving any changes, which comes in handy when you have opened a file to check something and you want to keep the file the same as it was when you opened it. Here's how you can close a file without saving any changes you have made on purpose or accidentally:

1. Select Close from the File menu.

2. If Elements asks you if you want to save any changes, click No on the dialog box.

3. The file will close, and any changes you made will not be saved.

Keep Track of Your Files

Even though Elements has the handy File Browser to help you find a file you have lost track of, it's a good idea to make your image editing work time easier and less frustrating by devising an inventory process for your images. You do not need to come up with anything complicated or time consuming, but you do need something. Unless you need to keep track of hundreds of images or more, you don't need to buy image management software.

Keeping track of your files gives you the same advantages that keeping track of any kind of inventory does: You save time and frustration by finding files easily, and you don't have to spend money replacing lost files.

Here are a few tips for keeping track of your images:

- Make a folder for each project and create folders within the project folder to organize the digital elements—such as one for images and one for text. Do the same for each new project.

- Create a coding scheme for the image files for a given project that is memorable and descriptive. For example, Ch1-01 would be the first image for the first chapter of this book and Ch1-02 would be the second image in the chapter.

■ Make a list of the images you need for each project using a word processing or spreadsheet program. Include the image filename; the location on the hard disk or network; and the image resolution, file size, and file type. Periodically throughout a project, update the list and make a final version of the list when you finish the job. Refer to this list when you have to work on a similar project. Perhaps you can reuse some of the images.

■ When you see an icon in the browser window rather than a small preview of the image, that doesn't mean the file isn't there (see Figure 3-3). It just means that there is no preview version of the image for you to see. If you see the filename, go ahead and double-click the file icon. Your file will appear, I promise.

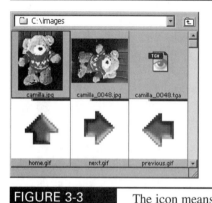

FIGURE 3-3   The icon means there is no preview of the image, not that the image isn't there

Add Information to Your Files to Help You Keep Track of Them

You know how you sometimes write something on the back of a personal photograph—maybe the date the picture was taken or the location? Isn't that a fast and easy way to keep important information about a picture? Well, Elements will let you do the same thing electronically. By using the File Info... feature, you can record information about an image, including a short description (anything you want to write), the copyright information, and the Web site location. If you took the picture with a digital camera,

Elements will automatically import information about the file from your digital camera, including the file size, the resolution, and the date and time the picture was taken—as long as your digital camera records this information when it takes the picture.

Here's how to add an electronic label, or caption, to an image.

1. Open the image in Elements.

2. Choose File Info... from the File menu. The Caption window opens.

3. Type in your description of the image.

4. Click Next to bring up the Copyright & URL section of the dialog box. Type in the copyright information and URL if the picture is located on a Web site.

5. If the image came from a digital camera and you want to check the specs on the image, click Next and specs will appear.

6. When you have finished adding all the information to the image that you want to save, click OK to close the window and save your work.

NOTE   *You can add file info to any image if you are using Elements on a Macintosh computer. If you are using Elements on a PC, you can add file info only to Photoshop, Photoshop Elements, TIFF, JPEG, EPS, and PDF files. That's because Macintosh files have resource forks that allow storing information from any file. PC files do not have resource forks, and thus only certain files can "package" file data along with them.*

TIP   *You can always view the information about a file after you have added it by opening the image and selecting File Info... from the File menu.*

Get Ready to Create a Contact Sheet

Another way you can organize your image inventory is by using Elements contact sheets. These contact sheets look exactly the same as contact sheets that photo development houses create and hand you with your stack of developed film. They are thumbnails (those small, stamp-sized versions of your images) arranged neatly on a sheet of paper for ready reference. In Elements, you can create your own contact sheets using the digital images already on your computer.

Since Elements looks inside one folder to create the contact sheet and grabs all the images in that folder to create the contact sheet, you may need to do a little rearranging of the file locations on your hard disk. Put all the files you want on one contact sheet—and only those files—in one folder.

 *If you add more files to the collection in the folder later, say, during the course of the project, you must create a new contact sheet from scratch to include the new files. Unfortunately, you can't simply add the new images to an existing contact sheet.*

Create a Contact Sheet

A contact sheet is something professional photographers use—and you have too, if you have asked the photo lab for the sheet of little pictures of your photographs. You do not need to have any files open when you create a contact sheet.

1. Select Automate from the File menu.

2. Choose Contact Sheet II from the menu that appears.

3. The Contact Sheet II dialog box appears. Tell Elements where to find the files you want to create a contact sheet from by clicking Choose.

4. Choose your contact sheet size, image resolution, and color type by either accepting the default settings or changing them to suit your needs in the Document section of the box. Since you're going to be looking at the images for reference purposes only, the default resolution of 72 dpi is a good choice. Anything higher is a waste of toner, really.

5. Choose the order in which the thumbnails will appear (across or down) and the size of each in the Thumbnails section of the box.

6. Change the font setting and size for the captions by making choices in the next section of the box. If you deselect the check box that says Use File Name As Caption, Elements will not use a caption for each image.

   When you make changes to the settings in the Contact Sheet II box, notice how the preview changes. In this example, I have changed the page size on this box so that I can print my contact sheets on tabloid-sized sheets of paper, as shown in the following illustration:

7. Click OK to start the process of creating your contact sheet.

8. When the process is complete, click the window to close the sheet and save it with a unique name that you will easily remember.

Once you create a contact sheet, you can print it to keep a copy for your files. The name of the file, but not the directory location or folder name, is printed when you opt for captions, so it is a good idea to write on the sheet where the files are located on your hard disk.

Another good idea, if others will be using these same images or working on projects that involve the images, is to make color copies of the sheet. Give a copy to everyone involved in the project so that they can learn what images are available and where they can be found.

Get Bigger Pictures in Your Contact Sheets

The default contact sheet layout puts 30 pictures on a page in six rows of five pictures each. That's a great idea if you've got lots of pictures to put on the contact sheets, but the pictures end up being really small. If your pictures look alike but have small particularities that set them apart, you may miss important distinguishing details unless you make the pictures bigger. Here's how to change the settings to get nine images, three rows of three, per sheet:

1. You don't have to open a file to set up a contact sheet, so, with a file open or without, select Automate from the File menu.

2. Select Contact Sheet II from the Automate menu; the Contact Sheet II window opens.

3. Go ahead and make all your selections and choices, including telling Elements where to find the files to use to make the sheets, but don't make any changes to the Thumbnails section of the box until the next step.

4. Type **3** in the Columns box and type **3** in the Rows box. Notice how the preview of the page to the right of the boxes changes when you enter these numbers.

5. If you want to make the images even bigger, deselect the box next to Use Filename As Caption and see how the images get bigger still on the preview. Without captions, Elements uses as much space on the page as possible to print the number of images per sheet you've selected (see the following illustration).

6. Click OK and Elements will start the contact sheet assembly process.

Elements will remember the changes you've make to the Contact Sheet II dialog box, so you won't have to re-create them next time you want to make a contact sheet.

Summary

In this chapter, I have told you a lot about how to open and close files in Elements, even when you are not sure what or where the files are. Plus, I have explained how you can use features inside of Elements to help sort and organize your files. Now it is time to move on and start learning how to edit images in Elements. In the next chapter, I will show you some easy edits you can make to entire images, such as how to fix a crooked scan.

Part II

Make Simple Edits and Adjustments to Images

How to:

- Straighten a skewed scan
- Brighten a dark image
- Bring out hidden details in images
- Make global changes to a group of photos
- Adjust color images to make them look realistic
- Create special effects quickly and easily
- Use filters to change an image

Even the most experienced professional photographers are sometimes dissatisfied with a photograph they have taken. Perhaps they were not able to get the exact shot they wanted or something unexpected happened to the film when it was developed. Maybe the image came back too light or too dark or there were shadows where there was supposed to be bright sunlight.

So, when you work with photographs, expect to have to do some work on at least a few of them after you import them. It's natural, it's normal, and you can make all the changes you need to make using Elements.

In this chapter, I will tell you how to make global changes to pictures—in other words, how to apply one or more edits to entire images. I will also tell you how you can look at an image and tell exactly what needs to be done to it to improve it and when to quit when you're ahead. Some pictures can be improved a great deal, while others can be improved only a little. You need to spend your editing time efficiently, working on images to improve them as much as possible and then moving on to the next when you've done all you can.

I also want to encourage you to pay attention to your graphic design instincts while making image edits, now and throughout the book. Elements places at your disposal digital versions of the traditional tools that photographers use to edit images, but you do not have to be a professional photographer to use these tools correctly. The tools are simple to use, and all you need to use them correctly is a little practice and your own instincts about what looks good and what doesn't.

Change an Image's Orientation

The needle in a compass points due north—at least when the compass is working, it does! Having the right orientation is important when you navigate so that you arrive at the intended destination. Paying attention to orientation is important when you work with images, too, if you are to communicate your visual message as you intend.

Orientation in images can mean correcting skewed images so that they lean neither to the left nor to the right. It can also mean changing orientation from left to right/right to left (flipping an image horizontally) or from top to bottom/bottom to top (flipping an image vertically—a mirror image).

Correct a Skewed Scan

When you scan an image, sometimes the image slips around slightly on the scanner glass. You may not even notice the problem while you are scanning, but later it is obvious that your picture is not pointing due north. You can fix such a problem the hard way or the easy way. The hard way is to scan the image again to try to correct the problem; the easy way is to let Elements correct the skew for you in a few seconds. No matter how badly off-center the scanned image is, you can fix it with Elements in a few steps. Here's how you can correct a skewed scan:

1. From inside Elements, open the skewed image file.

2. Select Rotate from the Image menu. A menu appears.

3. Select Straighten Image from the menu that appears and Elements straightens the image.

NOTE   *You can use the Straighten and Crop option on the Image menu to straighten a crooked scan, but if there isn't more than a sliver of white space around the image area, Elements will crop off part of the image when it straightens it to make it a rectangle. So, to be sure nothing is trimmed off, use the Straighten Image option.*

Flip an Image Horizontally

You can flip an image horizontally or vertically in Elements, but most of the time if you choose to flip at all, it will be horizontally, as shown in Figure 4-1. Since most images have an obvious top and bottom, flipping them vertically isn't useful unless you are trying to make an artistic statement (see Figure 4-2). You may choose to flip an image horizontally if you are using several images on one page and want to vary the orientation to create a set of images with greater visual variety.

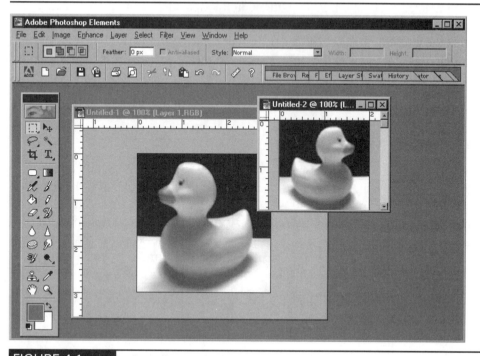

FIGURE 4-1   Some images look just fine when you flip them horizontally

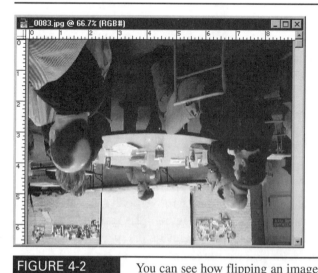

FIGURE 4-2   You can see how flipping an image vertically does not make sense for most images!

For example, say three images you want to use on one page show larger groups of people on the left than the right. Since changing the orientation of one of the images doesn't change the meaning, you could flip the second horizontally so that the larger group in this image now appears on the right. Here's how you flip an image horizontally:

1. Inside of Elements, open the image you want to flip.

2. Choose Rotate from the Image menu and a menu appears.

3. Choose Flip Canvas Horizontally from the menu and Elements changes the orientation of the image.

NOTE *If you want to flip the image vertically, follow the steps, but choose Flip Canvas Vertically in Step 3.*

How to ...

Draw Attention to an Image by Rotating It

It can be boring to keep your images on the straight and narrow all the time, so add a little variety to your images once in a while by deliberately rotating them a few degrees left or right (see Figure 4-3). Use this technique sparingly, though; it can seem as if you tried to make your images appear to dance across the page if you rotate each image a few degrees.

Here's how to rotate an image a few degrees to the left or right: With the file open on the screen, choose Image | Rotate | Canvas Custom and then when the Rotate Canvas box opens, enter a small degree of rotation (no more than 25) and click the button for left or right. When you close the window by clicking OK, Elements tips your image for you.

FIGURE 4-3   Rotating an image slightly can draw attention to the image more than not rotating it

Did you know?

Flipping an Image

You can flip an image vertically in another way by choosing Canvas 180° from the Image | Rotate menu. You can also push an image on its side by choosing either Canvas 90° Left or Canvas 90° Right from the Image | Rotate menu.

Make the Most of a Bad Image

Most of the time when you call a photograph a bad image, you are not talking about its behavior! It's just not all that you hoped it could be—it's too dark, it's too light, or important details aren't easy to see. All is not lost, though. You can reform every bad image in Elements to some degree.

If you are starting out with a really bad image, such as a snapshot of a black Lab puppy sitting in front of a dark brown door taken on a really cloudy day without benefit of flash—well, maybe the best you'll see is a few more details when you lighten the image. Still, it's worth the time to try to get the most out of your images. In this section, I'll tell you how to improve the usability of images that are too dark, are too light, or don't show all the details you know are there.

Brighten a Dark Image

We have all seen photographs taken in a room without benefit of a flash attachment or in a dark room with a flash that was not bright enough to lighten up the scene for the camera. You know, these are the photographs that remind you of cookies that were left too long in the oven and have come out a little too dark. Elements makes it easy to lighten up too-dark images. Here's how you do it:

1. Open the file in Elements.

2. Choose Fill Flash from the Enhance menu. The Fill Flash box appears.

3. Move the box, if necessary, so that you can see all (or most) of your image.

4. Make sure the Preview box is checked so that you can preview the effects your changes will make.

5. Move the slider from the left to the right, pausing momentarily to see the effect.

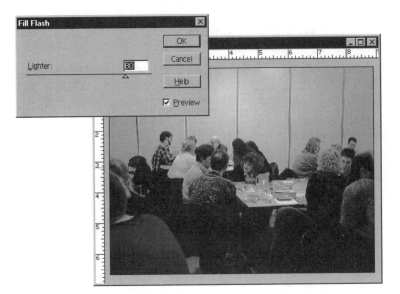

6. Keep moving the slider left or right until the image is as bright as you want it to be.

7. Click OK to close the window and apply the brightening effect to the image.

 *You can also control the amount of brightness you want to try on the image by typing a number in the box above the slider. If you have a really dark image, try **50** and work your way up or down from there as needed until you get the look you want to keep.*

Did you know?

A Few Degrees Brighter

Photographs usually look darker when they are printed or photocopied than they do onscreen. Make your images a few degrees brighter than what looks okay onscreen if the images will be printed on a printing press or reproduced on a photocopier. Add a few more degrees of brightness if they will be imaged on colored paper.

Darken an Overly Bright Image

If you have been to the beach or the pool lately, you may have seen some people you thought have had too much sunlight. Unlike people, though, images that get too much light don't tan or burn; they just look way too bright. They get that way because there was a lot of light in the room or the area where the photographs were taken or because there was too much light coming from a flash. You can make a too-bright image darker in Elements by adjusting the backlighting. Here's how you can correct an overly bright image:

1. Open the image in Elements.

2. Select Adjust Backlighting from the Enhance menu and the Adjust Backlighting box appears.

3. Move the box out of the way so that you can see most, if not all, of the image.

4. Make sure the Preview box is checked so that you can see what effect your changes will have as you experiment in the next step.

5. Move the slider to the right or type in a number in the box above the slider bar to make the image darker. Move the slider to the left to make the image lighter if needed.

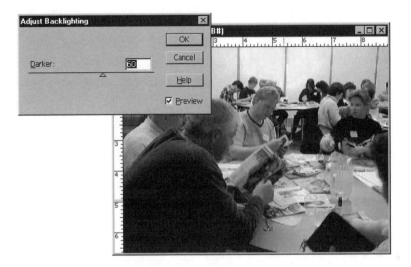

6. When you have darkened the image adequately and you are happy with the look, click OK. The window closes and Elements applies the darkening effect to the image.

Bring Out Hidden Details in Images

Sometimes after you have made an image darker or lighter, the correction still isn't enough to reveal all the details in an image. Or, maybe the image is a little out of focus. To bring out the details in an entire image, you can use two of the filters. Here's how you use these filters:

1. Open the image in Elements and select Sharpen from the Filter menu.

2. Select Sharpen from the menu that appears to bring the image slightly more into focus. Elements applies the effect to the image. If the image is still not focused enough, repeat this step as many times as needed.

3. Select Sharpen from the Filter menu and select Sharpen Edges from the menu that appears. Repeat this step as many times as needed, but more than once or

twice will probably accentuate the edges more than you want. The following is an image overly sharpened for demonstration purposes. Try something less extreme than what is shown here:

 *If the photograph is really out of focus, you can move the sharpening process along more quickly by choosing the Sharpen More filter the first or second time rather than using the Sharpen filter. The Sharpen More filter is a little more powerful than the Sharpen filter.*

Did you know?

The Screen Versus the Printer

The changes you make with the Sharpen filters will be much more obvious onscreen than they are when they are printed, particularly if you have the images printed on a printing press. The reason that you see such detail onscreen and apparently lose it during printing is that the screen has a much lower resolution than the printing press. The higher the resolution, the smaller the dots that make up the image and the less obvious the sharpening effect will appear. So, you may want to make the edges really obvious when you are going to have your photographs printed.

Fine-Tune the Level of Detail in an Image

Traditional photographic editing techniques include a process called unsharp masking, which, in the hands of a skilled technician, can really bring out the details in an image. In Elements, the Unsharp Mask filter allows you to adjust the settings on the sharpening capabilities to get precisely the level of detail you want. Since previews are built into the process, all you need to use the tool successfully is a little time to experiment. Here's how you can use the Unsharp Mask filter to fine-tune the level of detail in an image:

1. Open the image in Elements and choose Sharpen from the Filter menu.

2. Choose Unsharp Mask from the Sharpen menu. The Unsharp Mask box appears.

3. Make sure the Preview box is checked so that you can get a preview of the changes as you experiment with the settings for this filter.

4. To zoom in on the area shown in the preview window, click the plus sign beneath the window. To zoom out so that you can see more of the image in the window, click the minus sign.

5. If you want to see another part of the image in the preview area, place the cursor anywhere on the image such that the cursor changes into a hand shape. While holding down the mouse button (left button on a Windows PC), push the hand around until you see the portion of the image that you want to see, as shown here:

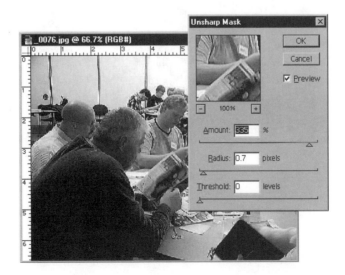

6. Adjust the Amount slider by moving the slider to the right, which increases the amount of edge detail you can see in the image. Keep moving the slider until the image edges are as sharp as you want them to be. If you are not sure where to start the process, type **100** in the box above the slider and move backward and forward from that point until you are pleased with the results.

7. Continue to work on bringing out details by adjusting the Radius slider upward a little at a time. Adobe recommends a setting between 1 and 2 for images that will be printed on a printing press, less for images that will be used at lower resolutions.

8. Unless you want to set the filter so that it looks at less than all the pixels on the edge of objects in the image, leave the Threshold setting at 0.

9. Click OK when you have the sliders set so that you are pleased with the amount of detail in the image. The box closes and Elements applies the changes.

You can create special effects in your image by moving one or all of the sliders up to the far right-hand side of the range. To give this close-up shot of glass marbles a sci-fi look, I have set the Amount and Radius at 100+ levels. I created the following image using the Unsharp Mask filter with high settings:

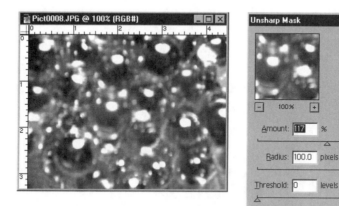

Did you know?

Shades of Gray

The Unsharp Mask filter looks for areas of the image where one color or shade of gray changes into another and then increases the amount of contrast between these areas.

Make the Lights Light and the Darks Dark

Sometimes an image isn't too dark and it isn't too light, but it looks a little muddy—that's not a technical term, but it conveys the concept, doesn't it? If your photograph looks a little dull or if you have a lot of lights and darks in the same image, you can improve the image's appearance by equalizing the tonal range in the image. You're really just adjusting the color or grayscale balance in the image, and here's how you do that:

1. Open the image in Elements and choose Adjustments from the Image menu.

2. Choose Equalize from the Adjustments menu that appears.

3. Elements automatically adjusts the tonal range of the image. There! The lights are lighter and the darks are darker!

 If you would like to nudge up the lightness and push down the darkness a little more, you can first equalize the image and then adjust the brightness and contrast a little using the procedure that follows.

Adjust the Shades in an Image to Improve Its Overall Appearance

Earlier in this chapter, I told you how to darken an overly bright image and lighten one that is too dark. I've also told you how to quickly change the tonal range. Here's another way to quickly improve an image that looks just slightly off when all the image needs is a little boost or reduction in brightness and contrast:

1. Open the file in Elements and select Brightness/Contrast from the Enhance menu. The Brightness/Contrast box appears.

2. Make sure the Preview box is checked so that you can preview your edits.

3. Slide the Brightness slider to the right to make the whole image brighter—as if you had applied a mild bleach solution to the image!

4. If the image needs to be a little darker, move the Brightness slider to the left.

5. Slide the Contrast slider to the right to add contrast to the image. Notice how this can make the image look brighter as well. Use the lowest Contrast setting you can; otherwise, you can erase edge detail with this tool.

6. Slide the Contrast slider to the left to reduce the amount of contrast in the image. Notice when you do this how the image gets darker overall.

7. When you have found a combination of Brightness and Contrast settings that you like, click OK. The box closes and Elements applies the changes to the image.

How to ...   Adjust Contrast in One Step

Here's a quick fix to bring out a little detail by adding some contrast to the image. Use this procedure when the brightness of an image is fine and all you want to do is bring out a little detail: Open the image in Elements and choose AutoContrast from the Enhance menu. Elements automatically adjusts the contrast for you.

How to ...   Quickly Perform a Brightness/ Contrast Adjustment

Open the image and select Auto Levels from the Enhance menu. Elements makes the adjustment and you can use the procedures outlined if you are not completely happy with the changes it has made to the image.

Fine-Tune Your Brightness and Contrast Settings

If you would like even more control over the change in Brightness and Contrast settings in your image, you can adjust these settings to a very high degree. Most of the time you won't need to use the technique that I am going to outline, but it can be useful if the Brightness and Contrast controls aren't giving you the effect you are looking to achieve. Here's how to fine-tune these two settings:

1. Open the image in Elements and select Brightness/Contrast from the Enhance menu.

2. Select Levels from the menu that appears and the Levels box opens.

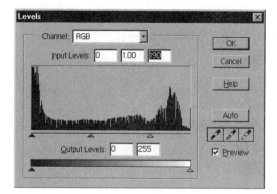

3. Slide the left slider until it is under the highest point on the left side of the graph.

4. Slide the right slider until it is under the highest point closest to the right side of the graph.

Here is another way to adjust the lightness and darkness of an image:

1. Click the first eyedropper and click the part of the image that is the darkest object.

2. Click the middle eyedropper and click the part of the image that is nearest to the midtone or gray.

3. Click the third eyedropper and click the part of the image that is the whitest and brightest.

4

 *Make sure the Preview box on the Levels box is checked so that you can see the effects of your edits as you experiment. Notice that there is no Preview window in the Levels box. The changes you make appear in the image itself but are temporary until you click OK. Until you save the image, you can use the Undo feature (on the Edit menu) or the Step Backward feature (also on the Edit menu) to restore the image to what it was before you made the adjustments.*

How to ...

Undo All the Changes You Have Made to an Image

In this chapter, we've covered a lot of ways to quickly alter the look of an image. That's good—you should experiment with them all, but you might not want to keep all the changes. You can get rid of all your changes to an image in a few seconds by selecting Purge from the Edit menu and then selecting All from the menu that pops up.

Correct Color Problems

Whether you are printing in color or posting an image to your Web site, you want the colors in an image to be perfect—or at least as good as you can make them. Just as when the colors on your television aren't right, nothing is more immediately obvious in a still image than color problems. If the sky in a landscape shot looks more like purple rose than sky blue and the picture wasn't taken at sunset, someone is bound to notice. Ditto if the boss's auburn hair is reminiscent of the color of freshly shredded carrots!

Elements gives you several ways to correct colors in a color image so that you get colors that are more realistic and closer to the original. Try to balance the color in an image first, which is the first procedure I have outlined. If that doesn't help enough, try altering the color and purity of the color in the image (second procedure). Then if the image still needs some help, try looking at different color variations (the third procedure). Maybe you will find a variation you prefer over the present image. Still not happy? It may be time to discard the color altogether (the fourth procedure) and turn the color image into a grayscale one.

Balance Color to Make Images Look More Lifelike

You know it's time to adjust the color on your television when the Caucasian skin tones look too orange. Or maybe everyone is looking slightly green. You know when the color is off in your TV. Use your color sense for still images like photographs, too. If the color balance is off in your photographs, try fixing it using this procedure:

1. Open the image in Elements and select Color from the Enhance menu.

2. Select Color Cast from the menu and the Color Cast Correction box opens.

3. Move the box out of the way so that you can see all or most of the image. Make sure the Preview box on the Color Cast Correction box is checked.

4. Notice that the cursor has changed to an eyedropper. Follow the directions in the box and click in the area of the image that should be white, gray, or black. The image changes each time you click in one of these areas.

5. Click Reset if you lose track of your clicks; Elements will reset the image to how it looked before you started this procedure.

6. Keep clicking in the image until you get the color balance the way you want it to be. Click OK to close the box and apply the changes to the image.

Make the Most of the Colors in Your Image

If you have tried the procedure just outlined and you still don't like the color balance, try this one next:

1. Open the image in Elements and select Color from the Enhance menu.

2. Select Hue/Saturation from the menu that appears and the Hue/Saturation box appears.

3. Make sure the Preview box is checked and the Colorize box is not checked. Move the box out of the way so that you can see all or most of your image.

4. Click the down arrow and select the color that you want to adjust from the list that appears.

5. Move the Hue (the word means color) slider to the left or right until the colors in the image are more to your liking.

6. If you desire, move the Saturation slider to the right to make the colors in the image more intense, to the left to weaken them.

7. Your hue and saturation changes may have made the image too dark or light. So, if you wish, move the Lightness slider to the left or right to compensate.

8. When you are satisfied with the color changes, click OK. The box closes and Elements makes the changes to the image.

NOTE
If you want to adjust the colors in the image separately or just adjust a single color, click the down arrow in the Hue/Saturation box next to where it says Master and select the color you want to edit. Then adjust the sliders. The effects may be subtle because you are adjusting only a single color at a time this way, but adjust the color too much and the changes will really stand out!

Make Quick Color Choices

1. Open the image in Elements and select Variations from the Enhance menu.

2. Elements opens the Variations box and presents a gallery of samples of your image with various color variations. The image and the current pick are the same at this point.

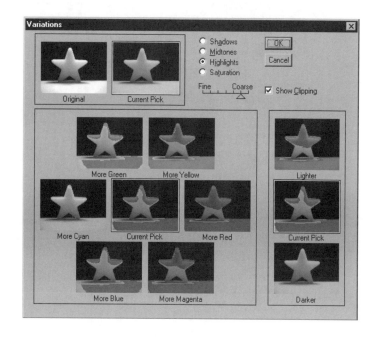

3. To check out the different changes that Elements can make, click each of the four categories at the top of the box (Shadows, Midtones, Highlights, Saturation). To speed up your color editing process, Elements shows you a gallery of possible color adjustments.

4. Adjust the Fine/Coarse slider to the left or right. Moving it left reduces the effect; moving it to the right enhances the effect.

5. To pick a lighter or darker version of the image, click the appropriate version of the image on the right-hand side of the box.

6. Click OK when you have made your image choices. The window closes, and Elements applies the effect to your image.

You can have a lot of fun "turning up the color volume" on your image and make some significant changes in your image in a few moments. Here I lightened the image and changed the color to add a lot more magenta. It even looks good in grayscale.

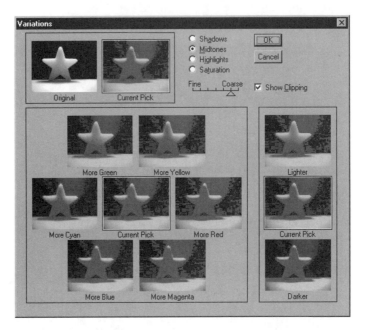

NOTE

Clipping is automatically selected when the Variations box appears. When this box is selected, some areas of the different variations may turn a neon color like yellow or red. These colors have not been added to your image—they are only there to show you the areas of the image that would be converted to pure white or pure black if you selected that particular preview.

Remove the Color from an Image

1. Open the image in Elements and select Color from the Enhance menu.

2. Select Remove Color from the menu that appears.

3. Elements automatically removes the color from the image and leaves behind shades of gray.

When you use the Remove Color feature, you are not changing the type of image from an RGB or indexed color image to a grayscale image. The image type remains the same as it was initially (the Elements default for color images is RGB). If you want a true grayscale image because you want to print your image using black ink only, do not use the Remove Color procedure; you must follow this procedure:

1.   Open the image in Elements and choose Mode from the Image menu.

2.   Select Grayscale from the menu. A box asking you if you want to discard the color information appears. Click OK and Elements automatically converts the image to a true grayscale image.

4

Photographic Special Effects

I wanted to tell you in this chapter about all the ways Elements lets you fix entire images. So far I've told you about how to fix even some bad images. But what do you do to fix images if all the other methods I've told you about so far just aren't helping enough? Well, then it's time for a little creative remedial work. You may need to change the look of the image entirely using some of the fast and easy special effects in Elements.

These special effects are a lot of fun to experiment with and can help you make the most of even the worst of photographs. They are also a lot of fun to use on boring, but otherwise fine, photographs. Who says photographs have to look like fresh-from-the-camera snapshots all the time?

Each of these following projects uses procedures I have told you about earlier in this chapter, so you can get some practice to reinforce what you've learned or just have some fun with your own photographs (see Figure 4-4)!

Make a Photo Look Like a Civil War Relic

1.   Open the image in Elements and use the Image | Mode | Grayscale command to make it a grayscale image.

2.   Use the Enhance | Brightness/Contrast control to adjust the brightness and contrast until the image looks dull and faded.

3.   Apply the Dust & Scratches filter to the image (Filter | Noise | Dust & Scratches).

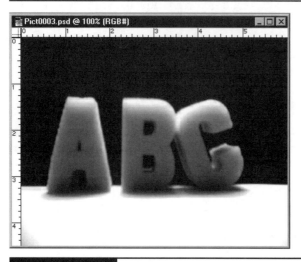

FIGURE 4-4   Here's my starting point for each of the projects

4. Apply the Add Noise filter to the image (Filter | Noise | Add Noise).

5. Convert the image to an RGB file (Image | Mode | RGB Color).

6. Adjust the yellows in the image to give it a sepia or brownish tone (Enhance | Color | Hue/Saturation and select Yellows from the drop-down list).

You can make any picture look a lot older by using this process. There are some other ways to accomplish the same result, and I will tell you about one of them in Chapter 8.

Create a Neon Glow Effect

1. Open the image in Elements and select Adjustments from the Image menu.

2. Select Gradient Map from the menu and the Gradient Map box appears.

3. Click the down arrow next to the color bar at the top of the window and a pop-up gallery of fills appears. Choose a fill in the middle or the end of the gallery to get the most colorful ones.

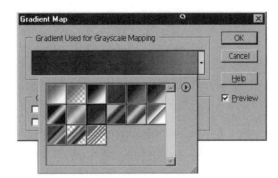

4

4. Click one of the really colorful fills to select it.

5. To experiment with possible fills, click several fills. When you have found the one you like best, click OK.

6. Elements applies the fill effect to your image, and you've got a neon glow in seconds.

Color changes like these are really good ones for any images that you will be using for children's and young adults' projects.

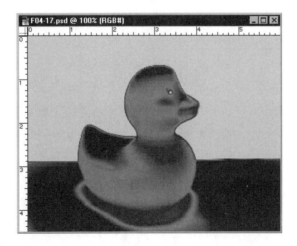

Change Colors in an Image from the Inside Out

You can take one image and make its direct color opposite by inverting the colors. You could also create a series of images that all contain the same elements but have different color schemes by taking one image, applying a different fill, as outlined earlier, for each version, and then applying this procedure to each of the new, neon images (see the color insert for examples of this process).

You can use this technique to create compelling and unusual images by turning the color tables on people. They expect to see one color, such as a yellow rubber ducky, yet they see something completely different. That makes the image memorable.

To turn the colors in an image inside out and replace them with their opposite colors on the color wheel:

1. Open the image in Elements and select Adjustments from the Image menu.

2. Select Invert from the menu.

3. Elements automatically inverts the colors in the image.

A Filter Sampler

Before I close out this chapter, I want to briefly mention how you can use filters to change the look of an entire image in a few seconds. I will tell you a lot more about filters later, but for now I want to show you a few of them in action.

To add even more of an antiqued look to my photo, I worked with the "Civil War relic" image I created earlier in this chapter and made it look like a sketch by using the Brush Strokes/Ink Outlines filter. Figure 4-5 shows the results of applying this filter.

To add a handmade look to any picture, you can apply the Texture/Mosaic Tiles filter. Figure 4-6 shows the application of this filter to the grayscale inverted image I worked with earlier in this chapter.

FIGURE 4-5   The Brush Strokes/Ink Outlines filter adds an antiqued look to photos

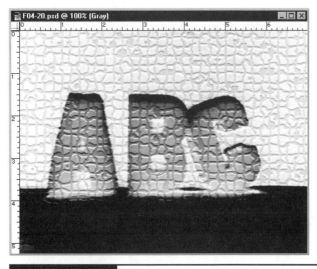

FIGURE 4-6   The Texture/Mosaic Tiles filter adds a handmade look to any image

For Figure 4-7, to give the original image a textured fabric look, I applied the Stylize/Tiles filter first and then the Distort/Ocean Ripple filter.

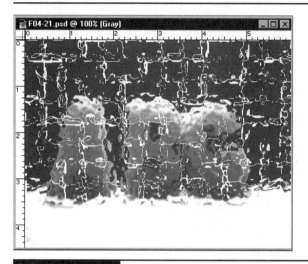

FIGURE 4-7   Here are two filters combined: the Stylize/Tiles filter first, and the Distort/Ocean Ripple next

Summary

Well, what a chapter! We've learned a lot about the tools and processes for making simple, yet compelling, changes to images. We've worked with scanned images, brightened them, changed the contrast, and, overall, worked to bring out the best in the images. You can use all of the techniques I've covered in this chapter to help you make the most of the photographs you have and will take in the future.

Chapter 5

Easy Spot Edits for Images

How to...

- Tell Elements what part of an image to change

- Remove red eye, dust, and scratches

- Attract attention to important parts of your images

- Adjust the focal point of your images

- Remove unwanted details

- Add artistic enhancements to parts of your images

In Chapter 4, I showed you how to make all kinds of global changes to your images—changes that affect the entire image. But what do you do if only part of an image is not what you would like it to be? Perhaps there are some scratches in a treasured photograph of your grandparents. Or maybe there is a touch of red eye in the deep brown eyes of the Vice President of Marketing in the photo you would like to use in the annual report.

Or maybe you liked some of the special effects in the last chapter and were wondering if you could apply one or more of them to only a part of an image. Well, I have good news for you. In Elements, if you can select it, you can affect it (by applying a special technique or filter). Your ability to select something is limited only by your ability to manipulate the various selection tools Elements offers.

In addition, Elements offers the digital equivalent of several traditional photographic editing techniques that you can use to alter the appearance of your images. As with all the tools and techniques in the software, you do not need to be a professional photographer to use the Burn, Dodge, Sponge, and other retouching tools.

In this chapter, I will show you how to select one or more portions of an image so that you can fix trouble spots or use any of the techniques you learned in the last chapter. I will also tell you how to rid your images of those pesky troublemaker image problems that mar otherwise good images. Good-bye red eye! Good-bye scratches! And, because I can't resist the reference to *Macbeth*: Out, out, wretched, telltale spots!

Get Ready to Make Specific Edits

Before you can make any changes to a portion of an image, you have to tell Elements what part of the image you want to change—otherwise, you'd be making a global change. That makes sense, right? So will the various methods you can use to select portions of an image, once I have explained how to get ready to make an edit by selecting a region of the image.

Unless you are using the Red Eye Brush tool, which has its own selection process, you can select a portion of an image that fits within a rectangle (with the Rectangular Marquee tool) or an oval (with the Elliptical Marquee tool). Using the Lasso tool, you can select any portion of image that you can draw around the edges of. First, I want to show you how to select part of the image using one of the geometric shape selection tools.

Make the First Pass

In this project, I want to show you how to select part of an image so you can tell Elements what portion of the image to edit. This is a basic procedure that you will use many times once you learn it.

1. Open the image in Elements and move around in the image until you see the portion of the image that you want to edit. Zoom in or out as necessary until you can see all of the area you want to select.

NOTE   *Hold down* OPTION *and* CTRL *and click the plus (+) key to zoom in or the minus (–) key to zoom out.*

2. Click the Rectangular Marquee tool on the toolbox and the cursor turns into a small cross shape. Click in the image area near the area you want to select.

3. Holding the mouse button down, drag down and to the right or left to select the area. Notice that Elements gives you a scrolling marquee (yes, that's where the name of the tool comes from) to indicate what portion of the image you have selected.

4. When you see that the marquee completely encompasses the area that you want to select (and not a moment sooner!), release the mouse button. Notice that when you release the mouse button, the marquee is still scrolling, but it has more white in it, as you can see here:

How to ... **Start Over**

You can remove the selection you have made by holding down CTRL on your PC keyboard and then hitting the D key (CTRL-D). Or you can click the new selection icon on the Options bar and then click in the image and select a new area. The previous selection marquee disappears and the new selection marquee appears.

NOTE *To switch from the Rectangular Marquee tool to the Elliptical (oval) one, right-click (PC only; single-click on the Mac) the small triangle in the corner of the Rectangular Marquee tool and a small menu opens. Select the Elliptical Marquee tool from the list and the icon on the toolbox changes to an oval shape. Once you have changed tools, the selection process is the same as it is with the Rectangular Marquee tool.*

How to ... **Use the Lasso Tools to Capture Irregularly Shaped Portions of an Image**

The Lasso, Polygonal Lasso, and Magnetic Lasso tools work the same way as the geometric shape selection tools. The only difference is that you click to start the selection process, follow the shape of the object as if you were tracing it, and click to end the selection process. Personally, of the three, I find the Magnetic Lasso easiest to use because it automatically finds the edge of the area you are trying to select—so you don't have to be as careful with this tool as with the other lasso tools.

You may have to zoom in so you can see the edges of the area you want to capture with one of the Lasso tools, so go ahead and zoom in to the level that you can see every pixel you want to edit (View | Zoom In). I have given you an example of the zoom in Figure 5-1.

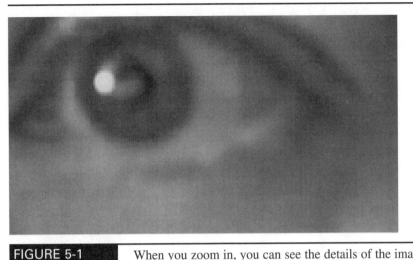

FIGURE 5-1   When you zoom in, you can see the details of the image more easily

   To switch between the three lasso tools, right-click (PC only; on Mac just click) the small triangle on the icon and a list of tools appears. Click the one you want to use and the icon on the button changes to reflect your selection.

Enlarge the Selection Area

It can be difficult to select just the area you want on the first pass, so Elements gives you a number of ways to refine the boundaries of the selection area once you have created a selection. I have told you how to remove the current selection so that you can start over. Now I want to tell you about a powerful feature that allows you to add to the current selection area or create multiple selection areas in one image.

1. With the image open in Elements, click one of the geometric selection tools. Click in the image and select an area. The selection marquee appears.

2. Click the Add to Selection icon on the Options bar. The cursor changes to a cross shape with a smaller cross shape on the lower right side. You can also hold down SHIFT and click and drag inside the selected area to activate the Add to Selection feature.

3. Click in the area of the image that you want to add to the current selection. If you overlap your selection area with the existing one, Elements incorporates the two into one larger selection. If you click an area that does not overlap the existing selection, Elements makes another selection area separate from the first.

NOTE   *If you click the Subtract from Selection icon, you can remove selection areas from your previously selected area. You can create some sophisticated selection areas this way, such as a rectangular shape with scalloped edges. Another way to make such a selection area is to have Elements select only the areas where multiple previous selections intersect. You do that by making multiple selections and then clicking the Intersect with Selection icon.*

How to ... Feather the Edges of the Selection Area

While you are learning about making selections, you can also change how the edges of a selection area appear. The default appearance is a clean cut that looks as if you cut the area out with a pair of scissors. However, you can feather the edges so that they look less distinct by increasing the Feather setting on the Options bar. You can also change the Feather setting after the selection is made by selecting Feather from the Select menu and typing in a higher or lower number.

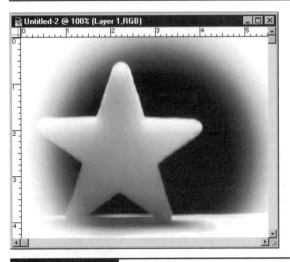

FIGURE 5-2   I have set the Feather setting at 15, much higher than the typical setting of 2 or 3; notice the effect around the edges

Remove Red Eye

Despite the fact that many cameras come with a flash that is specifically designed to ward off red eye in images, if you work with candid shots of people (as opposed to carefully lit shots done in a light-controlled studio), you will see lots of red eye in images. It is caused by light reflecting off of an individual's eyes, and I see it more in photographs of infants, children, and pets than in other kinds of photographs. Here is how you can eliminate the red eye in any image:

1. Open the image in Elements and zoom into one of the eyes that you want to remove the red eye from; make sure to zoom in enough that you can see some of the pixels in the portion of the eye where the red appears as well as the portion of the eye that is the correct color.

2. Click the Red Eye Brush tool on the toolbox. The cursor changes to a circle with a small square in the middle.

3. Choose a brush size from the Options bar. I like to use a brush size that is roughly the size of one of the pixels I am going to edit. That way, I don't accidentally color part of the area around the pupil itself.

4. Position the square right over the portion of the eye where the red eye is. You'll know when you've positioned it correctly because the Current Color box turns red. Click the red area to tell Elements that is the color you want to remove (the target color).

   I have zoomed in on this eye and have clicked the Red Eye brush tool; notice what the cursor looks like and how the Options bar looks after I have done this.

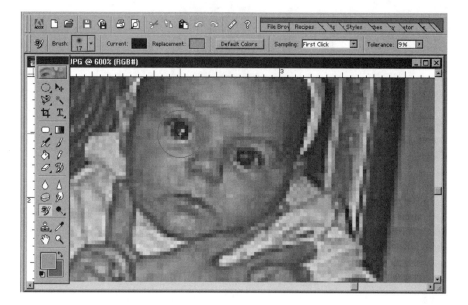

5. Now tell Elements what color you want to replace the target color with by clicking the Replacement Color square. The Color Picker box opens. Click the color you want to use to select it.

6. Hold the mouse button down and click the pixels in the area you want to change.

 If you have a lot of red eye to remove, consider using several shades of the same color because rarely are human and animal pupils a solid color—usually there are shade variations that you can see when you look closely.

7. If you find you are not able to change all the pixels, experiment with a smaller brush size and a slightly higher tolerance setting. To change the tolerance setting, type a higher setting in the Tolerance box on the Options bar.

8. Repeat the process for the other eye—when one eye is chock-full of red eye, the other one usually is too!

How to ...   Change Someone's Eye Color

Here's something fun that you might want to try with some of your personal pictures—not with some business ones. You can change the color of someone's eyes by following the same procedure you use for removing red eye. The only difference is that the target color is the current eye color and the replacement eye color is the new color. You can experiment with different eye colors and even give each eye its own color!

Eliminate Dust and Scratches

Older photographs, especially those that have been passed from generation to generation without benefit of special care, often end up a little scarred. If your family photos or even older photos from your company's distant past are looking a little worse for wear, you can repair them with a little effort. You don't want to make them look as good as new, because a little old-age patina is nice to see in older photographs. But you do want to make them look like they have been lovingly cared for over the years!

1. Open the image in Elements and click the Rectangular Marquee tool.

2. Select an area of the image where the image flaws appear. If there are lots of problems with the image and it's a small image, go ahead and select the entire image. Otherwise, just select one of the areas you want to repair.

3. Select the Dust & Scratches filter from the Filter menu (Filter | Noise | Dust & Scratches) and the Dust & Scratches box opens. Make sure the Preview box is checked.

4. Move the image area around or zoom in and out in the Dust & Scratches preview window until you can see most or all of the damaged area you are trying to repair.

5. Move the Radius and Threshold sliders in small increments backward and forward. Moving them in too large increments can blur the selected area so much that it doesn't match the rest of the image.

6. Click OK when you are satisfied with the repair work you have done on this section. The box closes, and you can see the results of your work in the image.

7. Repeat steps 1–6 for every area of the image you want to correct.

Bring Out Specific Details

In Chapter 4, I showed you how to bring out the details in an entire image with a few mouse clicks. You can do the same thing to one or more portions of an image by first selecting the area you want to emphasize and then sharpening the edges in that area. I have used this technique to attract attention to a specific area of an image. Here's how to sharpen areas of your image:

1. Open the image in Elements and click the Sharpen tool on the toolbox. The Options bar for the tool appears above the image.

2. From the Options bar, select a brush size and shape.

3. Choose a brush mode other than the default of normal if you want to change the appearance of the edges as you sharpen them. Click the down arrow next to the Mode box to open a list of settings.

4. To change the intensity, increase the Pressure setting by typing a higher number in the Pressure box or by clicking the right triangle and moving the pop-up slider to the right.

NOTE *Think of the effect of this parameter change as what it looks like when you bear down hard with a pencil. The higher the Pressure setting, the firmer and bolder the edge change is.*

5. Click the part of the image that you want to accentuate and trace the edges of the objects in that area or paint the area with the sharpening effect.

In the following illustration, I have gone over the edges of the duck and increased the pressure to show you what effect these changes can have on an image:

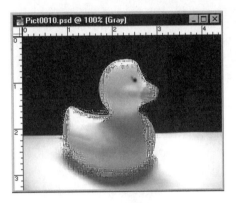

Add Depth to Your Image

Your hair can be flat and lifeless—especially if you are using that inexpensive shampoo again (shame on you!). Your images can be listless, too, without any definition or interest. What you need to make your hair perky is to switch to a new shampoo; you need to give your images a good wash to liven them up, as well. Here's how to add some depth and texture to dull images:

1. Open the image in Elements and decide which parts of the image you want to draw attention to and which you want to slightly obscure. Usually I pick foreground objects to emphasize, but you can experiment with different combinations.

2. Click the Sharpen tool and follow the steps outlined previously to roughen up some of the parts of the image. Use the Darker mode on some elements and

the Lighter mode on others. Change the pressure on some of the changes, too, in order to add more visual interest.

3. Click the Blur tool on the toolbox. The Options bar for this tool appears.

4. Go over some of the areas you have sharpened with the Blur tool. Notice how the area you sharpened and then blurred does not go back to the original appearance.

5. Use the Blur tool to blur areas near the sharpened areas. Vary the Mode and Pressure settings on this tool as you work—the settings and mode of operation are the same as the Sharpen tool.

6. Change the brush size for the Blur tool depending upon the size of the area you want to edit. Experiment with the irregularly shaped brushes. You can see what I have done here:

 I have found this one combination of techniques (sharpen and blur) to be a real gold mine of image editing possibilities. So often we see images that are ho-hum and mundane. I admit that making the most of these techniques takes some experimentation, but within five to ten minutes any image can take on new depth and interest.

Fix the Focal Point (Method #1)

Picture a scene in a movie: a well-dressed couple sitting at a table for two in a restaurant. A spotlight over the table shows every detail of their faces and hands. You see only the couple and the glittering silver on the table. Everything outside the pool of light is slightly obscured by darkness. You see everything that matters and nothing that doesn't.

As every good director knows, every good image (still or moving) needs a clearly defined focal point—the portion of the image that attracts your attention first. In really good images, you come away with an impression of little else. Well, as we know, not every image is a good one. In some images, it is hard to find the focal point. Or the focal point of the image is there, but it is something you would rather not have people notice. One way to move the focus to where you want it to be is to darken the areas of the image you don't want people to notice:

1. Open the image in Elements and select the Burn tool from the toolbox. If you don't see the tool, that's because the Dodge tool is the active tool at the moment. Right-click (PC only; Mac users single-click) on the small triangle at the lower-right edge of the tool and select the Burn tool from the pop-up list that appears.

2. Notice that the cursor shape has turned into a circle. Choose your brush from the Options bar that appears. Pick a brush size that is just large enough to allow you to work quickly, but not so large that it slops over into areas you don't want to edit.

3. Begin to paint the areas of the image that you want to obscure. To darken all the areas, you may need to change the Range setting from Midtones to Shadows and Highlights.

4. Change the Exposure setting by typing in a new number or bringing up the slider by clicking the right triangle and moving the slider control. The higher the setting, the darker the effect.

5. Keep working until you get the effect you want (see Figures 5-3 and 5-4).

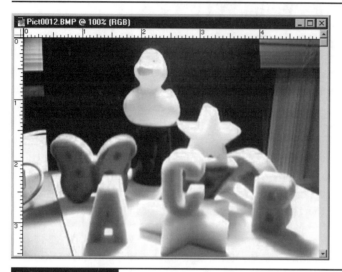

FIGURE 5-3   Here is the before shot: notice the window-frame molding and other elements in the background

FIGURE 5-4   Here is the after shot: I have used the Burn tool to darken the background almost completely

Fix the Focal Point (Method #2)

As I showed you earlier, you can drape darkness over the parts of an image that you want to obscure, and what is left becomes the focal point. You can further strengthen the focal point area of the image by brightening that area so that you get greatly increased contrast between the light and dark areas of the image. This technique builds on the one you just learned about adding darkness to an image:

1. Open the image in Elements and darken the background using the Burn tool.

2. Switch over to the Dodge tool by clicking the small triangle in the lower right-hand corner of the Burn tool icon and selecting the Dodge tool from the pop-up list that appears.

3. The Options bar for this tool appears.

4. Choose one of the smaller spatter brushes, such as Spatter 12 pixels, from the Brush palette.

5. Change the Range to Shadows and increase the Exposure to 50% or higher.

6. Click the lighter areas of the image near the focal point areas and gently outline the edges of the elements in the focal point area with the Dodge tool.

7. If there are lighter areas near the focal point area, brighten those up by clicking in them and scrubbing them a little with the Dodge tool (see Figure 5-5).

FIGURE 5-5   Here is the original shown in Figures 5-3 and 5-4 after I have used this technique on it

5

Paper Over Part of an Image

We have talked about shifting the focal point and removing details of an image to hone in on exactly what you want people to see. But what if you like part of an image and want to use it again somewhere else in an image? You can use part of any image to create a wallpaper effect in your image. Here is how to take a piece of an image and reproduce it again and again:

1. Open the image in Elements and click the Clone Stamp tool.

2. The Options bar for the tool appears and the cursor turns into a circle.

3. Make your brush size and type selections from the Brush palette. Leave the other Options bar settings as they are for now.

4. Hold down ALT and click in the segment of the image you want to clone. The cursor turns into a stamp shape. On the Mac, hold down APPLE/COMMAND and click.

5. Click in the area of the image that you want to paper over and drag back and forth to paint the image with the copied area. Keep painting and Elements will reproduce the entire image as if a copy had been layered and then moved slightly as to be offset over the original. If you want to apply only the part of the image you clicked and that the brush area covered, deselect the Aligned box before you make your stamp.

6. Release the mouse button when you have covered over the unwanted elements.

NOTE   *You can change how the Clone Stamp works by selecting one of the many modes available when you click the down arrow next to the Mode option. Experiment with them and see what effects they have (see Figure 5-6). If you make the Opacity lighter, you can get a translucent effect when you stamp the cloned part of the image.*

Enhance Images Further with Unique Spot Edits

Not every image you work on will have major problems that you need to edit out of existence. So, I wanted to let you know you can add interest to portions of your images in several ways. A little touch-up can brighten any image. Plus, you may want to use one or more of the approaches I have outlined thus far to remove troublesome problems and then use the spot edits outlined in the following procedures to add some additional interest to your images.

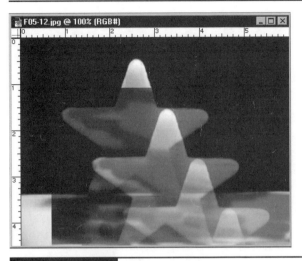

FIGURE 5-6   In this image, I have taken part of the star in the center of the image and cloned it a few times

How to ...   **Add New Details to Your Image**

You can add details to your image by using the Clone Stamp tool as I described in the last section, but you can also add brand-new details to the image in another way. You might want to use the Pattern Stamp tool to add depth to an image or to outline an area. There really is no limit to the ways you can use this tool; once you have seen it in action, you will come up with some interesting ways to use it.

With your image open in Elements, right-click the Clone Stamp tool icon and select the Pattern Stamp tool from the list that appears. Choose your brush and make your mode and opacity changes as you did for the Clone Stamp tool. Now, choose your pattern from the selection options that appear when you click the down arrow next to the Pattern option. Paint your image with the new pattern. Switch as many times as you want! Figure 5-7 shows the same star image I used for the Clone Stamp illustration with a few patterns painted on.

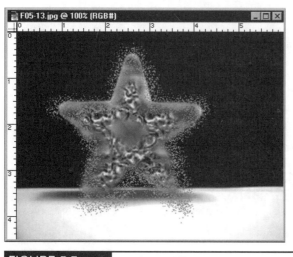

FIGURE 5-7   What a difference it makes to an image when you do this!

Draw Puddles in Your Image

I admit it—putting puddles in your image is not an enhancement you are going to use every day, but it is so cool that I did not want to close out the chapter without telling you about it. How many times when you were a child did you dump some paint out on a piece of paper and play with it by running your fingers through it? Even if you didn't, how many times have you looked at a modern art painting and wondered if the artist had not done exactly that? (See Figure 5-8 for some fun I had with puddles.) Here is how to make your image look as though you had fun doing some finger painting:

1. Open the image in Elements and click the Smudge tool.

2. Make your brush, mode, and pressure selections and changes on the Options bar.

3. Click in the image and, holding the mouse button down, swirl the tool around to create puddle effects in the image.

4. Click somewhere else in the image and repeat Step 3 to add another puddle.

FIGURE 5-8   Here's an image I used earlier with lots of puddles added

Color Wash Your Image for a Unique Look

Interior designers use color washes all the time to give elegant, yet simple, new looks to rooms all through the house. You can do the same thing with your images to give them a special designer look of their own. Using a color wash on your images is also a good way to help different elements blend together more smoothly, particularly if you have combined different looks using the tools in the earlier sections.

You can use this effect on the entire image simply by washing it, but I like to use it only on portions of an image. It is a particularly effective technique to use when you want to use color to highlight a grayscale image. You use it by selecting a color and using it to lightly tint a portion of the grayscale image. Here is how to give your images a new look with a color wash:

1.   Open the image in Elements and click the Sponge tool. Notice that the cursor changes to a circle and the Options bar for the tool appears.

2.   Make your brush, mode, and pressure selections on the Options bar. To remove color from the image, use the Desaturate mode; to add color to the image, use the Saturate mode. The higher the setting on the pressure, the darker the color wash will be.

3. Double-click the Foreground Color square at the bottom of the toolbox and the Color Picker box appears.

4. Click the color you want to use for your color wash effect.

5. Click OK to close the box.

6. Hold the mouse button down and swish the color over the area you want to highlight. Keep swishing until you are happy with the new look of the image.

Summary

What a wild ride! We have spent a lot of time looking at the various ways you can make images look different. You've learned to remove red eye, smooth away scratches, and copy parts of images. There was a lot in this chapter, but now that you've learned the material, it's time to move on to learn about other ways to change how images look.

Chapter 6

Quick Trims for Better Images

How to:

- Increase the Wow Factor of your images

- Remove unwanted details in images

- Delete the background of an image

- Make new images from old ones

- Add visual interest to images

In Chapter 5, I showed you how to make images look better, and one of the ways you can do that is by adding something to them—a little darkness or a little detail goes a long way. In this chapter, I want to tell you how to make your images better by taking things away from them and how to use the principles of subtraction to construct new images using parts of another.

No matter what kind of image you are dealing with—amateur or professional—you will find from time to time that an image has too much in it. It could be something small such as the portion of a plant you see at the bottom right of Figure 6-1. It could be something major such as a whole group of people. Whatever it is, the image would look better or be more useful to you if you removed it. You can make these surgically precise edits easily in Elements. I want to show you the fastest, easiest ways to make subtractive edits using the tools in Elements.

I also want to show you how easy it is to stretch your image inventory by combining simple edits with creative image transformation techniques in Elements to come up with new images. In a few steps, you can create the kinds of images you would have to pay hundreds of dollars for if you bought them from a stock photography company. Plus, I want to show you how to have fun with your images after you've trimmed away the excess and removed the unnecessary.

The picture in Figure 6-1 is a great image: a happy bride and groom standing in front of a marvelous old stone arch. The only problem is, when I took the shot, to get it from this (the best) angle, I had to include a little of the greenery in the foreground. Not to worry; in this chapter I'll show you how to remove the problem.

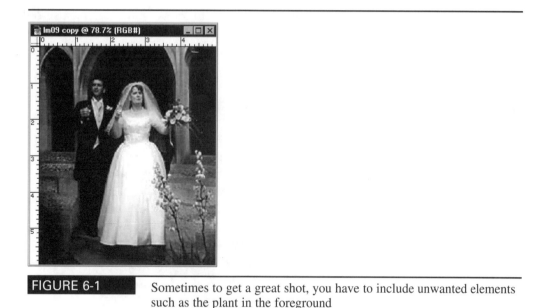

FIGURE 6-1   Sometimes to get a great shot, you have to include unwanted elements
such as the plant in the foreground

Crop an Image to Increase Dramatic Impact

Before you trim away part of an image, it helps to study the image for a few moments
to locate the parts of the image that you can do without and those you must keep.
When you are trying to heighten the dramatic impact of an image, you can usually do
without a lot more than you think you can. I will show you what I mean in the
examples that follow, but first let me walk you through the process of trimming
an image:

1. Open the file you want to edit in Elements.

2. Click the Rectangular Marquee tool on the toolbox. The cursor changes to
    crosshairs, and the Options bar for this tool appears above the image area.

3. Change the Feather amount to 0 by typing **0** in the Feather box.

4. Click one of the corners of the area of the image that you want to keep.
    Holding the mouse button down, select the entire area of the image you want
    to keep.

In the following illustration, I only want to focus on the two men seated at the table, so that's the area I have selected. Before you trim your images, pick an area of the image that you want to keep and trim until you have only that area left.

5. Select Crop from the Image menu and Elements removes the part of the image outside the selected area.

6. Save the trimmed image and use a name other than the original so that you do not overwrite the original file. You may wish to use that original image again, so you need to save it in its unedited state.

You can see the results of my trim in the following illustration. Notice how the trim has changed the meaning of the image: now you see two men listening intently instead of a group of people looking off into nowhere.

Eliminate Unwanted Details

So, now we can tackle the problem of the extraneous vegetation that cropped up (sorry, couldn't resist the pun) in my shot of the bride and groom. I want to show you several ways to eliminate unwanted details. I could crop the image, as I showed you how to do, but I would have to crop so much of the image that I would eliminate much of the stone arch and, as a result, much of the character in the image. So, I will show you how to slice away a segment of an image and replace it with another part of an image.

Part One: Remove Parts of Your Image

Sometimes a picture is fine except for one or two details. If those details weren't there, the image would work beautifully for your purposes. Don't pull out the scissors when Elements has so many ways to remove unwanted portions of an image. Here's one way to remove parts of an image:

1. Open the image in Elements and select the Rectangular Marquee tool.

2. Select the part of the image that you want to remove that does not overlap with the part you want to keep. Zoom in to that area of the image if it is a small portion of the image (see the following illustration).

3. Select Cut from the Edit menu and Elements removes that portion of the image, leaving the rest intact.

4. Click the Eraser tool on the toolbox. The cursor changes to a circle, and the Options bar for the tool appears above the image.

5. Zoom in until you can see the pixels in the area of the image that you want to remove.

6. If necessary, change the size and type of the brush so that you can work quickly and efficiently. Use a smaller-size brush if you are working right up against the edge of the part of the image you want to keep. Use a larger one to erase larger portions at a time.

Part Two: Substitute Another Image for What You Remove

We have to put something into the image to replace the area where we removed the plant. In my example image, I opted to copy the portion of the stairs next to the groom.

1. With the image open in Elements, select the portion of the image you want to copy.

2. Click the Clone Stamp tool.

3. ALT-click the portion of the area you want to copy. (It's OPTION-click on the Mac.)

4. Click the area you want to stamp and fill in the rest of the image with the copied image material.

Following is the example image without the plant. The finished, edited image highlights the bride and groom, and the plant material no longer detracts from the image's main focus.

Remove the Background of an Image

I want to show you how to quickly remove the background of an image using several tools in Elements. If you know how to remove the background from an image, you can reuse the foreground elements in other images or drop another background in to replace the original one. This simple technique can be very useful once you have learned how to do it.

It is, however, much easier to use this technique when the background is distinctly different from the foreground, especially when the colors are different. If the foreground and background are much the same color, this technique is more difficult to use, but you can use it to remove most of the background. I will tell you how to remove more of the background later in this chapter.

1. Open the image in Elements and select a portion of the background.

2. Choose Similar from the Select menu. Notice how Elements automatically increases the selection area to include all contiguous areas of the same color.

3. Choose Grow from the Select menu. Elements increases the selection area again.

4. Repeat Steps 2 and 3 until Elements has selected as much of the background as you can get it to select without selecting any of the foreground objects. See the following illustration to see how I selected the whole background:

5. Select Clear from the Edit menu. Elements deletes the selected area.

    To better show the result of this technique, the image on the left is the stars without the background and the one on the right is the former background of the image after I pasted it into another file (see the following illustration).

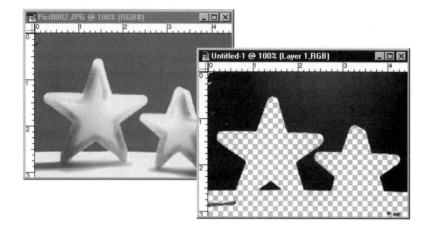

6. To render the trimmed area transparent and finish the removal of the background, select the Magic Eraser tool from the toolbox and click anywhere in the clipped background area. The area turns into a checkerboard, indicating that the background is now transparent. If any areas of background color remain, click those areas.

7. Choose Deselect from the Select menu to turn off the selection.

8. Save the new, background-less file with another name than the one you started with. This is always a good idea when you are doing extensive edits on an image. You never know when that original will come in handy!

NOTE   *If you want to trim away the background and copy that trimmed piece to the Clipboard, substitute Edit | Cut for Edit | Clear. Elements will copy the background to the Clipboard, and you can paste it into this image or into another one.*

Fun and Easy Edits Using Quick Trims

Elements gives you some easy-to-use tools to quickly remove any unwanted portions of your images—people, plants, you name it. You can even cut away the whole background of an image in just a few minutes. But I don't want to close out this chapter without showing you a few of the fun things you can do with quick edits. Let's start with one image (see Figure 6-2) and see what we can do with it.

FIGURE 6-2   This is the before image I used for all the projects that follow

How to ...   **Remove the Last Traces**

Sometimes when you use the technique I just explained, you find some lingering traces of the background color around the edges of the foreground objects. If you are working with color images, you need to clip those off before you use the foreground objects in another image. If you don't remove the last traces of the background color, the color can show up as thin halos around the edges of the objects when you use them again. Here's how to remove the last snippets of background.

Open the image in Elements and remove the background using the technique just outlined. Zoom in on the image until you can clearly see the remaining bits of color around the edges of the image. Click the Background Eraser tool on the toolbox and click an area that you want to erase. Carefully erase the pixels that you do not want to have in the image.

Construct a Patchwork Quilt from an Image

This procedure can give you a wide range of new looks for an image if you combine it with some of the filters. I have used a filter at the end of the procedure to show you what I mean.

1. Open the image in Elements and check the image size (Image | Resize | Image Size).

2. Resize the image if necessary so that the width and height are the same.

3. Click the Rectangular Marquee tool.

4. Click the down arrow next to the Style box and select Fixed Size from the pop-up list that appears.

5. Enter a width and height that create either a square or a rectangle. The dimensions must divide evenly into the total height and width of the image.

6. Click the portion of the image that you want to use to create your quilt square. Notice how Elements constrains the size of the selection area to the dimensions you have chosen.

7. Select Copy from the Edit menu.

8. Create a new file with a transparent background and a dimension or size as large as you want the quilt to be (File | New).

9. Paste your square into the new file by selecting Paste from the Edit menu.

10. Repeat Steps 5, 6, 7, and 9 until you have enough squares for your quilt. You can vary the size of the quilt squares by changing the size of the selection area.

11. Slide your squares around in the new file until you have a complete quilt.

12. Apply a filter if you want to finish off the new image.

Following is the quilt. I filled the alternating rectangles with color so that I could have some solid areas to the quilt. I did this by filling the background with a solid color and pasting the squares on top.

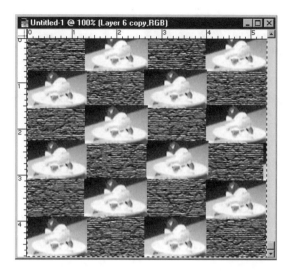

Create Three Images from One Original

All you need to create three new images from one original is to find three pieces of the image that would work by themselves as separate images. Take the following procedure and repeat it three times. But it's not like three wishes and that's all you can get—repeat the procedure as many times as you wish.

1. Open the image in Elements and select the area you want to make into a new image.

2. Select Crop from the Image menu. Elements cuts away the rest of the image.

3. Save your new image with a new name.

4. Select Step Backward from the Edit menu and the original image reappears.

5. Remove the current selection by selecting Deselect from the Select menu.

6. Repeat Steps 1–5 as many times as desired!

Figure 6-3 shows the three images from one original, now put together so that you can see their original relative positions.

FIGURE 6-3   The three images

Spin Out a New Image

Here is an unusual way to create a new image, but think of all the fun you could have with your company logo. You will not be sorry if you take the few minutes to try this:

1. Open the image in Elements and clip off a portion of the image.

2. Select Liquify from the Filter menu. The Liquify box opens.

3. Click in the center of your image and stroke outward. Curve the stroke a little as you go or leave it straight. Just choose one type of stroke and repeat it.

4. Continue to stroke until the entire image is liquified (see the following illustration).

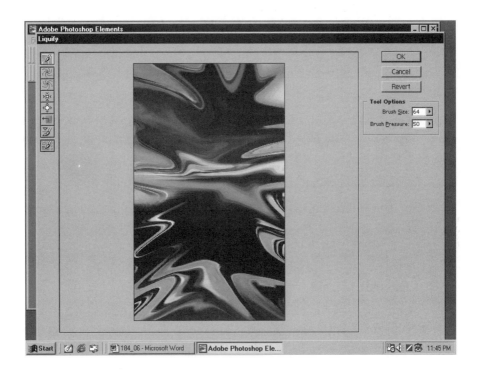

5. Apply the Twirl filter (Filter | Distort | Twirl).

6. Crop the new image so that you can see only the inner part of the spiral.

In the previous illustration, I cropped the woman from the center of the original image and put her through the Liquify process. In the following illustration, you can see the completed image. Can you believe I got something so artistic looking by starting with the image of a woman I cropped from the original image?

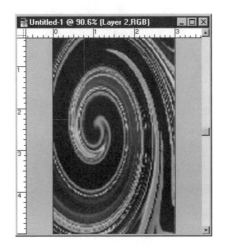

Add Visual Interest with Scalloped Edges

This technique is a good way to add interest to images you might use in a newsletter or any informal correspondence such as a photo you want to dress up a little to send to a friend.

1. Open the image in Elements and select the Elliptical Marquee tool from the toolbox. Notice how the cursor changes to a cross and the settings appear on the Options bar.

2. Change the Feather amount by typing **10** in the Feather box.

3. To keep your ellipse the same proportions all the time, select Constrained Proportions from the pop-up list that appears when you click the down arrow next to the Style box.

4. Click Add to Selection so that Elements will remember all the selections you are going to make.

5. Moving around the edges of the image, draw selection areas all around them. Do not worry if the selection area doesn't cover a small portion of the outer edges. You can go back and repeat the selection process until you've selected all the edge area that you desire.

6. When you have finished selecting all the areas, select Clear from the Edit menu and Elements gently slices away the edges. Since you feathered the edges, they look transparent. Following is a finished sample image:

Make a Web Site Banner

Banners are prominent features on Web pages. You can create your own and have them color coordinate with the images on the page. Here's how to create your own Web site banner using a portion of a photograph.

1. Open the image in Elements and select the Rectangular Marquee tool from the toolbox.

2. Select a wide, thin strip from a part of the image. The more colors in the resulting strip, the better.

3. Select Crop from the Image menu so that only the selected area is left.

4. You can use the selection as is or apply a filter to disguise the objects in the strip. I used the Crystallize filter (Filter | Pixelate | Crystallize) for my example. The larger the crystal size, the less obvious the original details are. I used a size 10 because that's the size I wish I were!

5. Use the Image Size controls to resize the image to your requirements (Image | Resize | Image Size).

Following is a background for a banner for your Web site created from the original image shown earlier. Notice how it's hard to make out any details from the original image.

Summary

In the last two chapters, I kept you busy adding material and subtracting material from images to make them look better. In the next chapter, we will take all this a step further and I will show you how to combine objects from different images and different images to make entirely new ones.

Part III

Make More Sophisticated Changes to Images

Chapter 7

Combine Images

How to:

- Duplicate a whole image

- Combine image objects into one new image

- Whip up an image layer cake

- Create a multilayered image collage

- Construct a panoramic image

- Weave image fabric

- Make your images glow

In Chapters 5 and 6, I showed you how to make simple edits and use the various selection and trimming tools in Elements to make images look better. Now that you know how to improve and remove objects from your photographs, it's time to learn how to put all the pieces together into something new.

In this chapter, I want to show you how to use the effects, fills, and layering capabilities of Elements to do things with images you probably never knew you could do so easily. You have seen some of these kinds of images before, but you probably thought they took hours and several kinds of software to create. The truth is, you only need a little bit of time to experiment and you only need Elements. All the example images in this chapter I created myself in less than 15 minutes per image.

I will also use techniques you learned in the earlier chapters of this book, but do not worry if you have not been reading sequentially. I will briefly explain how to do each step of the procedure even if I have covered it in detail in previous chapters.

Before you begin reading, you may want to gather up some prints or the electronic versions of some prints (scans, digital camera images) to look at while you are reading. Try to imagine using the techniques on your own images or follow along as I describe the techniques.

Turn One Image into Many

As I demonstrated a little bit at the end of the last chapter, one image can be the starting point for many different images.

In this section, I want to show you how to make complete duplicates of an image and then how to select and copy pieces of those images to make new images.

Copy an Image Electronically

Elements lets you make full copies in seconds without a photocopier—what could be easier when you want to make an electronic duplicate of an image?

If you want to edit an image, it's a good idea to work on a copy of the original image and leave the original untouched. Later, if you decide you do not like your edits or you make a mistake, you can always start over if you have edited the copy and not edited the original image! Here's how to make a duplicate of an image:

1. Open the image in Elements.

2. Select Duplicate Image from the Edit menu. The Duplicate Image box opens.

3. Elements gives the image almost the same name as the original, but it puts an underscore at the beginning and the word "copy" at the end of the name. Copy an image again, and it adds the underscore and "copy 2." You can change the name if you want to give the copy a radically different name.

4. Click OK to continue. Elements displays the copy of the image. You can tell because the name of the file in the title bar of the image changes.

5. Save the copied file (File | Save). You can also change the name of the file when you save it if you wanted to, but did not, when you copied the image.

7

NOTE   *Elements does not close the original image file when it makes a duplicate, so you can switch back and forth between the original and the duplicate by choosing the file you want from the list of open images that appears at the bottom of the Window menu. Switching back and forth is useful if you want to change the duplicate but take a look at the original once in a while as you work on the copy.*

Did you know?   **File | Save As**

You can also make a copy of a file by opening it and then saving it with a different name (File | Save As). Just make sure to change the filename in the Save As box before you click Save.

Construct a Collage

A *collage* is one image made up of parts of other images. You probably made them in elementary school art class. Making a few of them with images you cut out of magazines or with digital images is a good way to practice being creative with images. You can also use this technique to assemble an image for personal or business use. These kinds of images are guaranteed attention-getters!

Before you get started making a digital collage, you need to do the same thing you do when preparing to make a paper one—look through your images and find interesting pieces that will look good together. After you have done that, you're ready to start using Elements to clip out and paste those images together.

In this collage technique, I show you how to assemble a collage on one layer. Elements has this wonderful capability for creating layers in images almost as if you had stacked up sheets of transparent film one on top of another. By placing different elements on different layers, you can create many different looks (see Figure 7-1). In the second version of this technique (see Figure 7-2), I will show you how to create a layered collage using the same objects I used in the first collage—so that you can see the difference layers can make.

1. In Elements, create a new file (use the File | New command). Make the image area at least 4×5 inches to give yourself some room to work. Select a transparent background for the image.

2. Open the images you want to borrow objects from and select and copy the objects one at a time. (Use the Edit | Copy command for this.)

FIGURE 7-1   I combined several objects to create this collage

3. Paste each object into the new file you created in Step 1 by switching to that image and choosing Paste from the Edit menu.

4. To add some visual interest to your collage, pick a few filters and apply one to a few objects, another to a few more, and so on.

5. Move the images together so that they touch and none of the background is showing. If necessary, copy and paste more objects from the other images. Or, make duplicate copies of objects you have already brought into the collage.

6. Arrange some of the objects so that their edges appear to slide under one or more of the nearby objects. Click the object whose edge you want to slide under the adjacent one and select Arrange from the Layer menu.

7. Choose Send Backward from the pop-up menu that appears. The part of the selected object that intersects with the adjoining object disappears under the edge of the adjoining object.

8. Continue sliding objects around and tucking edges in here and there until you are satisfied with your collage.

Assemble a Layered Collage

Using the Send Backward command on the Layers | Arrange menu, you can create a limited layered look for your collage.

However, when you put different objects on different layers, you can really give an image a 3-D look because you can control precisely how objects overlap. Plus, as I will show you in this technique, you can change the opacity of a layer and thus make objects on that layer look solid or translucent.

1. Follow Steps 1–4 as just outlined, but select only one object to use. This object appears on your base layer.

2. Paste your next object (or several objects) into the image you are constructing while you are on this new layer.

3. Elements adds a new layer and switches to the new layer. You can see that the new layer has been added and the switch has happened because the name in the title bar of the image window shows the new layer name.

4. Repeat Step 2.

FIGURE 7-2   Creating a collage with layers lets you adjust the opacity of the layers

5. Choose Show Layers from the Window menu. The Layers palette appears. You can also click the Layers tab on the Palette box to get the Layers palette to appear.

6. Click one of the layers to select it and change the opacity to something less than 50%. You can change the opacity by typing a new number in the Opacity box or by adjusting the slider that appears when you click the triangle next to the Opacity box.

7. Click another layer and change its opacity to something less than 25%.

8. When you change the order of the layers, the look of the image changes. To change the order of the layers, click a layer and drag it below one or more of the other layers.

NOTE   *To delete a layer, click it and drag it into the trash can at the bottom of the Palette window. If you are not sure that you want to delete a layer, click the eye icon at the left of that particular layer's line in the palette. Elements slides that layer out of the stack temporarily but does not delete the layer. To see the layer again, click the space where the eye was. The eye, and the layer, reappear.*

Did you know?

Creating a Collage

You can create a collage using any object you can import into or create inside Elements. You could, for example, create a series of shapes using the drawing tools and use them to construct a collage or supplement one created with objects taken from photographs.

Create a Panorama Shot from Several Images

Nature photographers have created panoramic images for many years by taping pieces of film together and making prints from the film. It's a tedious process, and you can easily make mistakes. You can make panoramic images much faster with Elements. The program gives you a way to quickly stitch several images together into one solid sweep on an image. Here's how you do that:

1. Select the images you want to put together and put those files in the same directory on your hard disk. Put only these images in the directory.

2. Open Elements and choose Photomerge from the File menu. You do not need to create or open a file.

3. The Photomerge Setup box appears. Click Choose if your pictures are not located in the directory shown in the box and select the directory (folder) where the images are located. Click OK when you are done and you return to the Photomerge Setup box.

4. Leave the reduction percentage at 50% unless you are using large images, such as 8×10-inch originals. Elements has to reduce the images somewhat to fit them all together without running out of memory.

5. Leave the other settings as they are for now. Later on, I will show you what happens when you change these settings. Click OK to start the process.

6. Elements opens the images and sets them side by side in an image window. Then the Photomerge window opens so that you can edit the composition.

7

Elements places as many images as it can in the large white area in the window. Any that it could not fit it leaves in the smaller white area at the top of the window.

7. Rearrange the order of the images if you want to by clicking one and pushing it into a new position in the box below the smaller box at the top of the window. Click and drag any image in the smaller strips onto the work area below.

8. Move the images around as you would pictures set out on a table that you want to arrange in a straight horizontal line. When you are happy with your composition, as I am with the arrangement shown in Figure 7-3, click OK. Elements closes the window and opens an image window with the panoramic image in it.

9. Save the image by selecting Save from the File menu.

FIGURE 7-3   Here is my panorama of images

Cook Up a Layer Cake

The ability to create layers in an image is such a powerful tool, I could probably write an entire book about this feature in Elements alone! That's another book, though. In this one, I do want to offer you a couple of projects that illustrate some of the potential that layers can give you in constructing images. Here's how to create a layer cake out of portions of images. You can use this technique with any image or set of images, but I've chosen to use portions of an image I took of a bowl of glass marbles. You would not have known I started out with this one image if I had not told you.

1. Create a new file in Elements that is at least five inches square and has a transparent background.

2. Open the file (or files) you want to use to create the layers for your cake and select a rectangular section of the image. Copy the image and paste the layer into the empty, new file you created in Step 1.

3. Copy another rectangular strip from another image or another strip from the first image.

4. Paste the new strip into your layer cake image and move it so its bottom just touches the top of the other strip. Elements automatically creates a new layer and puts this strip on the new layer.

7

5. What's a cake without icing? Create a new layer, then double-click the Foreground Color square to bring up the color picker and click a color for your icing. Click OK.

6. Click the Paintbrush tool and paint some icing on your cake while you are on this new layer. Don't worry if your lines are a little sloppy—homemade cakes usually look a little sloppy anyway.

7. Next, switch to one layer of the cake by opening the Layers palette and clicking the layer you want to edit. Click off the views of the other layers and icing.

8. Apply a filter to this layer (try one of the Texture filters).

9. Repeat Steps 8 and 9 for the other two layers. Use a different filter each time if you are feeling really creative. Click the views of all the layers back on to survey your composition.

10. Slide the layers that hold the cake layers around to see if you like any other layer arrangement better (sorry, could not resist this pun!). Because your icing is on a separate layer, you can move the cake layers around without disturbing your icing!

You can create a layer cake with slices from one or more original images. I liked the shape that the marbles gave in the original image, so I used slices from one image to make my cake (Figure 7-4).

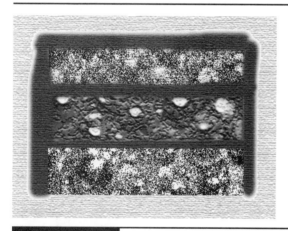

FIGURE 7-4   Here is my layer cake, complete with icing and filter-affected layers

Add Ghostly Details to Images

In this next example, I want to show you how to take an object from one image and layer it on top of another image to end up with a ghostly figure hovering in the background area. Once you understand how this technique works, I bet you will think up a dozen ways to use it right away. Think about putting images of people who couldn't come to your latest cookout or class reunion into a picture of the event and sending it to them (see Figure 7-5 for more).

1. Open the image in Elements that contains the person or object you want to turn into a ghost. Select and copy the part of the image you want to put in the other image.

2. Open the destination image in Elements and create a new layer. Set the opacity for the layer at 15%.

3. Paste the copied part of the other image onto this layer.

4. Adjust the opacity of the layer up or down until the image is the perfect level of opacity for the ghost effect you want to create.

5. Zoom in so that you can see the edges of the pasted-in objects and use the Blur tool to soften the edges a bit. Most ghosts do not have sharp edges, you know!

6. You can use the Sponge tool to lighten some of the areas inside the pasted area to give the ghost a more ethereal look.

FIGURE 7-5   You can use this effect to create a little whimsy in your images

Visually Enhance Your Image with Fills and Effects

Sometimes the most eye-catching images are the ones you have the most fun making. All the creative energy that you put into creating the image just comes spilling out when someone else sees the finished piece. I want to show you a few ways you can use the skills you have learned thus far in this chapter to turn out some really creative images.

Put Together a Visual Puzzle

The best kind of image to use for this technique is one that has objects in it that are easily recognizable if pieces of them are missing. In my example, I used an image with two stars in it. Using something instantly familiar such as a simple geometric object or a human face makes it easier for the person looking at the puzzle image to put the pieces back together mentally. If you use something less immediately recognizable, such as a crowd scene, the final image is not as impressive.

No matter what kind of image you choose, if you add a frame to the image before you cut it up, as I explain how to do in these next steps, you will give people a powerful visual tool for recognizing where the pieces go. To give even more visual clues, use a frame that is obviously a frame and made of a color that is not prominent in the original image.

1. Open the image in Elements and open the Effects palette by choosing Show Effects Browser from the Window menu or clicking the Effects tab in the palette well.

2. Choose one of the frame effects, such as the Wood Frame effect, and apply it to the image by clicking the thumbnail for the effect and dragging it over the image. Elements applies the effect so that you can preview the end result; click OK to apply the effect to the image. See the following illustration for an example of a wood frame:

3. Select Merge Visible from the Layer menu to glue the frame down to the image and make them both one layer.

4. Save the image with a new name before you proceed. You may want to use this image as the "answer" image later on or to start over again later if you would like to cut the puzzle up several different ways.

5. Click the Lasso tool and select an irregularly shaped portion of the image. Select Cut from the Edit menu.

6. Create a new file that is at least one and one-half times the dimensions of the original image. Choose a transparent background.

7. Paste the cut piece from the original image in the new blank image.

8. Repeat Steps 4, 5, and 7 until the original image has been cut to pieces and the pieces are all in the new image. Make sure to mix up the pieces—don't make the puzzle too easy!

9. Click some of the pieces and rotate them by choosing Rotate from the Image menu. Select Free Rotate from the pop-up menu and handles (small squares) appear on the object. Click one of the corners and rotate the puzzle pieces a few degrees left or right. I have rotated several pieces in my puzzle, as you can see here:

7

When you are finished making the puzzle, you can leave it as is and let people reassemble the image in their minds. Or, if you leave a lot of room between the pieces, you can print the puzzle out, trim away the background between the pieces, and have a real paper puzzle people could assemble.

Print out the original image if you want an answer image for people to refer to, and save the puzzle piece image.

> **NOTE**   *You can use any selection tool to cut the puzzle up with. If you were making a paper puzzle for little children, for example, you might use the Rectangular Marquee tool just to make the puzzle easier to solve.*

Weave Your Images Together into a Fabric Look

With the layering capability of Elements, you can create multilayer images as I have described earlier in this chapter. With a little more creativity, you can create layered images that look woven together. For my sample illustration, I started to create a fabric look by taking small strips on two images and weaving them together.

To create the two source images, I used a pattern fill for one fiber and then a solid color for the other. Then I treated the image fibers with filters to make them look more like fabric fibers. You could follow the same procedure and use two photographs or strips from one large photograph. Just make sure that your source fibers have lots of contrasting colors in them.

1. Create a new image in Elements and draw a rectangle that fills the entire image window.

2. Fill the image with a pattern by selecting Fill from the Edit menu. Click the down arrow next to the Use box and select Pattern from the pop-up menu that appears.

3. Click the down arrow next to the Custom Pattern box and a palette of pattern fills appears. Click one to select it.

4. Click OK and Elements fills the shape with the pattern (see the following illustration).

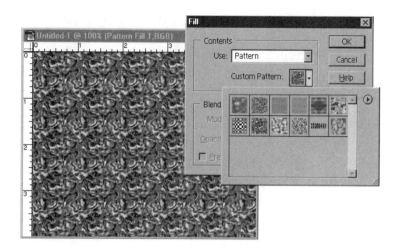

5. Cut a thin slice of the first box and paste it into a new, blank image window that is the same size or larger than the boxes you created. Cut another thin slice from the other pattern fill box.

6. Draw a thin rectangle about the same width and length as the strip and fill it with a color.

7. Simplify the drawn rectangle so you can apply a filter to it by selecting Simplify Layer from the Layer menu.

8. Have fun using filters to alter the appearance of the strands. Use the Liquify filter (Filters | Liquify) to noodle the lines around a little so that they look more like threads, as I have done and shown here:

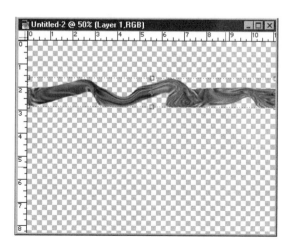

9. Duplicate the layers the threads are on by clicking each thread and selecting Duplicate Layer from the Layer menu. Push the threads apart and repeat until the image area is full of threads.

10. Select half of the threads (each color) and rotate them 90 degrees.

11. Arrange the threads so that some run underneath others by using the four menu selections that appear when you select Arrange from the Layer menu.

NOTE *Try doing this technique using threads you have applied the Neon Nights effect to before you start weaving.*

I left the weaving undone so that you could see how the fibers fit together (see Figure 7-6). If you create one layer with fibers running horizontally, another layer with horizontal fibers in different locations, and a layer of vertical fibers, you can slide the vertical fiber layer in between the two horizontal layers almost as a real weaver would do on a loom.

FIGURE 7-6   Use two contrasting threads to weave your image fabric

Use Fills and Effects to Add Interest to Your Images

Now that you understand how to make and manipulate layers and you have had a little fun using them, I want to show you how to combine the various fills and effects in Elements with various objects. In this section I am going to revisit some of the projects I showed you how to do earlier in the chapter and take them one step further.

Make the Edges of an Image Glow

You can apply glowing edges to any object in Elements in a few simple and quick steps. Adding an outer glow to an object makes it look as though light is spilling out from under the edges of the object. When you use this effect with some of the objects in a multilayered collage as shown in Figure 7-7, the effect is truly spectacular. Here is how to add a special outer glow to any object:

1. Open the file and select the object you want to set aglow.

2. Open the Layer Styles palette by selecting that tab from the palette well or by selecting Show Layer Styles from the Window menu. The Layer Styles palette opens.

3. Select Outer Glows by clicking the down arrow next to the box at the top left of the window and selecting Outer Glows from the list that appears.

4. Scroll through the thumbnails of available glow effects. When you find one you like, click it and drag it over the image to apply it. Elements applies the effect to the object.

7

 You can apply only one glow effect at a time. If you drag another effect over a glowing object, Elements replaces the old glow with the new one.

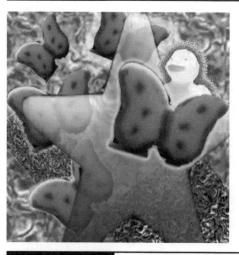

FIGURE 7-7   Here is the multilayered collage you saw a little earlier with a little outer glow applied

Create a Glow for Pieces of Your Image

You can also add a little glowing touch to the inside of objects, which results in a fun effect when you use the procedure that follows on simple objects. Remember our simple stars that you have seen throughout the book? In the sample image (see Figure 7-8), I took the ghostly image and added a little inner glow to the shape and, just to add a little more fun, added a drop shadow effect. Here's how to reproduce the look:

1. Open the image in Elements containing the object you want to add an inner glow to.

2. Open the Layer Styles palette by selecting that tab from the palette well or by selecting Show Layer Styles from the Window menu. The Layer Styles palette opens.

FIGURE 7-8   I gave the ghost from the example image I made earlier a little bit of an inner glow

3. Select Inner Glows by clicking the down arrow next to the box at the top left of the window and selecting Inner Glows from the list that appears.

4. Scroll through the thumbnails of available glow effects. When you find one you like, click it and drag it over the image to apply it. Elements applies the effect to the object.

5. Select Drop Shadows from the list on the Layer Styles palette. Scroll through and find one you like. Drag it over to the image. Elements applies the drop shadow to the object.

Create a Coordinating Shape to Accompany an Image You've Worked On

Once you create an image layer cake, you have to serve it, right? So, you need a coordinating cake plate to serve it on. In this example, I'll show you how to make a cake plate using pieces from the layer cake shown earlier. You can use this same procedure to create a shape to set off anything else you create. Here's how to use the layer cake to make a serving platter to go with it:

1. Open the image you want to use to create the plate.

2. Use the Pattern Stamp tool (click the Pattern Stamp icon and click the image) to sample a section of the image. Close the image.

3. Create a new image and draw a circle that is larger than the slice of cake you will cut.

4. Stamp around the edges of the plate with the sample of the cake image.

5. Fill the plate with a checkerboard pattern by choosing the checkerboard pattern from the custom fill palette and choosing Overlay from the Mode list that pops up when you click the down arrow next to the Mode box in the Fill window. Change the opacity to 50% to let the stamped areas show through a little.

6. Open the cake image and use the Polygon Lasso tool to cut out a slice of cake.

7. Paste the slice onto your cake plate. (See Figure 7-9 for the finished product.)

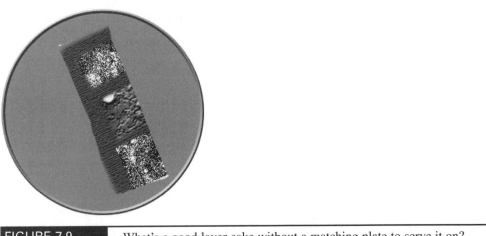

FIGURE 7-9   What's a good layer cake without a matching plate to serve it on?

Did you know?

Applying Effects to the Whole Image

You can apply many of the same effects that I have shown you how to apply to objects to entire images. You can also duplicate an image, drop it over another image as a complete layer, and adjust the opacity to about 15% and get a whole bunch of ghostly objects sprinkled over the base layer image.

Summary

I hope that in this chapter I have given you enough of a look at the ways you can combine images and change the look of various image parts to get you excited about what you can do with Elements beyond making simple edits and fixing some photographic problems like red eye. With Elements, you can be more creative than you ever thought you could be. In the next chapter, when you'll see how to use color to change how your images look, you'll learn ever more about the fun, creative power that Elements contains.

Chapter 8

Use Color to Change How Your Images Look

How to...

■ Add color to an image

■ Strip all the color from an image

■ Use color to attract attention

■ Color-wash an image

■ Color-coordinate your images

■ Create your own Impressionist painting

■ Frame an image

■ Create your own frame

Earlier in the book, I showed you how to correct the color in an image. You need to do that with any photographic image you want to use in print, in a presentation, or on the Web. In this chapter, I want to introduce you to the ways you can add color to an image and use colors to change images. Remember, though, that to get the most out of the procedures in this chapter, you should color-correct your images first.

To get you started, I've given you a few projects that are fun ways to learn how to use the color tools in Elements. It's a good idea, too, to learn more about the drawing and painting tools, so I've given you a few projects to show you more about them, as well.

Once you've learned something about the tools, do the projects in Chapters 7 and 9. I want to show you that, in Elements, you can use these tools to make your images look more interesting and artistic than you ever thought possible. There is an artist inside of you, no doubt!

When you are finished with the colorful projects, you may want to add a finishing touch to your images. To show you how to do that for your projects, I've given you step-by-step instructions on adding borders and frames.

Connect the Dots

"Connect the dots" is a staple of children's game and color books. It's a good way to teach them how to look for shapes in what appears, at first, like a jumbled mass of dots. I want to show you how to create a connect-the-dots image in Elements, not only to keep your kids happy on a rainy day, but also because you can use the same technique on business images. Think of using it for internal newsletter images or even corporate T-shirts.

You can use this technique on any image, but it's easier and faster to do when you pick something without a lot of small details. To prepare the finished image (see Figure 8-1), I used the double-star image I have used in various other images in the book.

1. Open the image in Elements and click the Pencil tool.

2. Create a new layer for the image. (Open the Layers palette by clicking the Layers tab in the palette well or using Window | Show Layers. Then, click the New Layers icon to create a new layer.) The icon looks like a page with the lower-left corner turned up (see the following illustration).

3. Click the new layer to select it and work on that layer.

4. Select a medium or large hard, round brush from the Brush palette by clicking the down-pointing triangle on the control panel next to the word "Brush." I chose a #19 for my example.

5. Select a color for your brush by double-clicking the Foreground Color box and clicking somewhere in the color window that pops up. (Later, I will show you how to switch to a new color.)

6. Click the edge of the image to create a dot.

7. Move around the edges of the image, clicking periodically to put down a dot. Place dots around the entire perimeter of the image.

8. Check to see if you have enough dots to make it possible to solve the puzzle by opening the Layers palette again and hiding the view of the background layer. (Open the Layers window and click the eye to the left of the background layer. The view of the layer disappears. To get it back, click the space where the eye was. The eye and the view of the layer reappear.)

9. Add more dots if you need them.

10. When you have enough dots, open the Layers palette again and click the background layer to select it. Drag it over the trash can icon at the bottom of the window. Elements deletes the layer, leaving your dot layer intact.

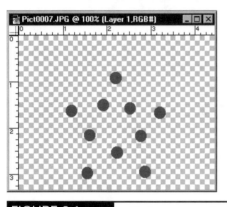

FIGURE 8-1   Grab your pencil and connect the dots!

Construct a Building Block

This project is another fun one for children to do on rainy days; if you leave off the colors, they can color the block in themselves. I will also show you how to apply color to each side of the block and let them add their own embellishments by hand, such as letters or small patterns.

You can also use the project in the office; how you use it is limited only by your imagination. I thought that 3-D blocks would look nice as graphics in a computer-generated presentation. Companies are always trying to build something, aren't they? Teams, products, territories...you get the idea.

1. Create a new file in Elements. Make it at least six inches on each side and give it a transparent background.

2. Click the Rectangle tool and draw a rectangle in the middle of the work area. (If the Rectangle tool is not visible, right-click the drawing tool that is visible and select the Rectangle tool from the list that pops up). Elements fills the square with the foreground color. That's fine, leave it that way for now.

3. Draw another rectangle directly above the one you just drew. Make this one the same width, but not quite as tall as the other one.

4. Change the color of the rectangle by clicking the color box (the box filled with the color of the rectangle). Click the slider handles on the color bar in the middle of the box and slide them up or down until you get to a new color you like. Click OK and the rectangle changes to the new color.

5. Get ready to skew the sides of the rectangle so that they angle away from the sides of the first rectangle (see the next illustration). Do this by selecting Transform Shape from the Image menu and then selecting Skew from the pop-up menu. Small, clear squares appear at the corners and midpoints of the edges of the rectangle.

6. Click the upper right-hand corner of the rectangle and drag right until that side of the rectangle is skewed slightly. Click the upper left-hand corner of the shape and drag it to the right in parallel with the other side.

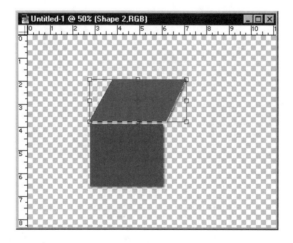

7. Draw a rectangle to the right of the first one. Make the new rectangle as tall as the first one, but not as wide. Fill the new rectangle with a different color from the first two.

8. Skew this rectangle so that its top and bottom slant upward and run parallel to each other. Match the slant of the sides of the second rectangle as I did for the finished image in the next illustration. You may have to adjust the skew of the second rectangle to make it match up neatly with the third rectangle. If you do, click the Move tool first so that you can select the second rectangle.

Did you know?

After you draw a rectangle (or any shape), you can fill it with a pattern instead of a color. Try this on one or more sides of the block. Click the side, select Fill from the Edit menu, and click the down-pointing triangle next to Custom Pattern. Click one of the small squares on the palette that pops up and Elements fills the shape with the pattern.

Remove the Color from an Image

Sometimes you will want to remove color from an image if you are going to print that image in a document that is only black and white. Turning the image into a grayscale image is a good idea even if you are going to print the black-and-white document on your office or home color printer. You get a better-looking image when you change the image type to grayscale before you print it.

You will also have to convert the image to grayscale if you are going to have color separations of a black-and-white document made so that the document can be printed on a printing press. If you don't change the image type to remove the color, the image won't show up properly on the color separation film.

Here's how to change the colors in an image to shades of gray:

1. Open the image in Elements.

2. Choose Mode from the Image menu.

3. Choose Grayscale from the pop-up list that appears.

4. A box with the question "Discard color information?" appears. Click OK.

5. Elements changes the colors to shades of gray and changes the image type to Grayscale.

6. If the image looks too light or too dark, adjust the contrast by selecting AutoContrast from the Enhance menu. If you are not happy with the results of the automatic correction, you can always adjust the brightness and contrast manually.

7. Save the grayscale image with a name that is different from that of the color image. You never know when you might need that color image again!

Attract Attention with Color

Color is a great way to communicate instantly. Just think about it: A bull runs toward the red flag. You stop when you see a red stop sign. You go when you see a green light or run toward the red Exit sign when that bull spots the red flag you're carrying!

Bold colors, especially when they are different from the surrounding colors, attract instant attention. You can use this visual reality to draw attention to all kinds of things, including a specific portion of an image. That's what I am going to show you how to do in this project.

For this project, you can use any of the three tools you can use to paint color onto an image in Elements. They are the Airbrush tool, the Paintbrush tool, and the Pencil tool. Each tool has its own distinct look, so you should experiment with them to see the different looks they can create.

1. Open the image in Elements and convert it to a grayscale image (see the preceding project).

2. Convert the image to an RGB color image so that you can add color to the image. Do this by selecting Image | Mode | RGB Color. The type of image changes, but the image looks the same as it did when it was grayscale.

3. Add a new layer to the image.

4. Click the Foreground Color square and choose a bold color by clicking it. Use the sliders if you need to get to another color.

5. Select a brush size and type from the Brush palette for this tool.

6. Pick something in the image to color and click it to start the coloring process. Clicking and dragging over the area of the image is how you color that part of the image.

7. Change to another color and brush and paint another small portion of the image.

Strengthen the Color Impact in Images

Color is wonderful, and we live in a color-filled world. Sometimes, though, you can have too much color in an image, and that abundance of color reduces the visual impact of the image. You can increase the color impact in an image dramatically in just a few moments inside of Elements. Here's how:

1. Open the image in Elements.

2. Select Adjustments from the Image menu.

3. Select Posterize from the Adjustments menu.

4. The Posterize window appears. Make sure the Preview box in the window is checked.

5. The default number of levels is 4. Change the number to 8. The more levels you put in the image, the more tonal ranges appear in the image. See the images (Figures 8-2 and 8-3) for two examples.

I want to show you the same image with more levels of posterization so that you can see the difference the various levels can make. Basically, in this image of two yellow stars, a level 4 posterization makes four levels of yellow. A setting of 8 for this image gives you eight shades of yellow.

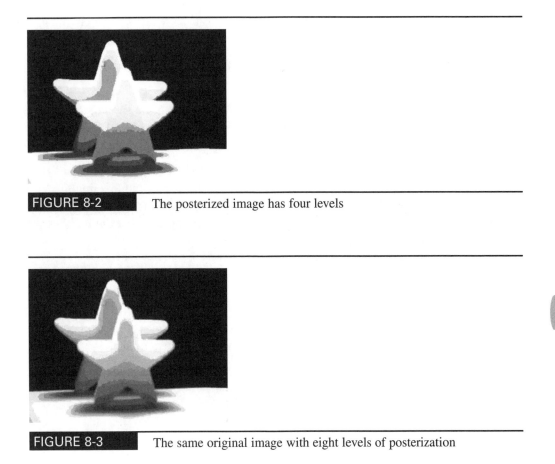

FIGURE 8-2	The posterized image has four levels

FIGURE 8-3	The same original image with eight levels of posterization

8

Split a Background

I am including this procedure because the students in my Photoshop class often ask how it's done. Once you see it done here, you will start to realize how many ads and images in magazines use this simple technique to give some color depth to images. In this example (shown in Figure 8-4), I have used a one-third/two-thirds division of the colored background, but you could use any division that you like. Half and half is another common division of the background.

1. Create a new image with a transparent background.

2. Click the Rectangle tool and draw a rectangle or square the size of the image background. Elements automatically puts the rectangle on its own layer.

3. Open the Layers window, click the layer on the window to select the layer, and change the opacity to less than 100%. I used 85% in the example image.

4. Click the Paint Bucket tool and click the rectangle. Elements fills it with the color set as the foreground color.

5. Draw another rectangle to cover one-third of the background area and Elements fills it with the same color. Change the opacity of this layer to something less than the opacity of the other rectangle layer, say, about 25%.

6. For some extra visual interest, apply the Marbled Glass effect to one or both layers. Do this by clicking the layer to select it and opening the Effects window (Window | Show Effects Browser or click the Effects tab in the palette well). Click the Marbled Glass effect and drag the thumbnail over the background you have created.

7. Elements will show you what the effect would look like and asks if you want to keep the effect. Click Yes to keep it; click No to go back to the original background.

You can save this background and use it as the bottom layer in another image. You can also copy and paste objects from other images into this image.

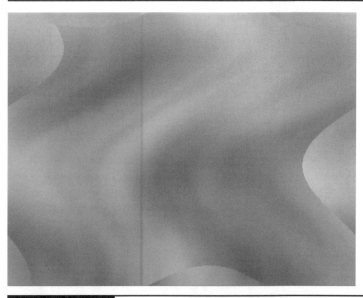

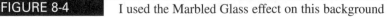
FIGURE 8-4   I used the Marbled Glass effect on this background

You can use two different colors, but if you are going to print the image on a printing press, where the two color layers overlap, the ink colors will mix and give you a color you may not like. To prevent this from happening, draw two separate rectangles that touch but do not overlap and fill each with the color you want to use. Figure 8-5 shows another split background.

8

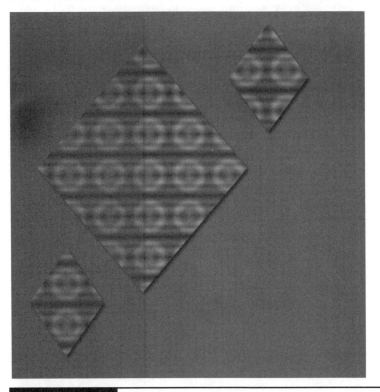

FIGURE 8-5   Look closely and you will see the split in the background

Age a Photograph

Okay, I know that one of the reasons you want to use Elements (probably) is to fix flaws in old images like your grandparents' wedding photograph. I've shown you how to correct a lot of the problems that come along with older photographs, such as scratches and dust. But making a new photograph look like it was taken decades ago at the dawn of photography can be a wonderful way to modify an image. It's fun to do with group shots and wedding portraits, and when you get finished, it's fun to print the images and select an old-fashioned frame for them. Here's how to age a photograph:

1. Open the image in Elements.

2. Select Variations from the Enhance menu. The Variations window opens and you can see different color versions of the image (shown next).

3. Make sure Midtones is selected at the top of the window. Click the variation labeled "More Yellow," since color photographs turn yellow over time.

4. Select Noise from the Filter menu and choose Add Noise from the Noise menu.

5. The Add Noise window opens. Set the amount of noise at something less than 10% to add a hint of age to the image. Click OK and the window closes.

6. Select Blur from the Filter menu and choose Blur from the Blur menu that appears. Elements slightly blurs the image.

In my final image, I only blurred the image a little (see Figure 8-6) by applying the Blur filter once. If you apply the Noise and Blur filters once or twice more, the image will look even older.

FIGURE 8-6   Who would guess this image is only a year or so old?

8

Apply a Color Wash

When you color-wash a wall, you take paint and dilute it with glaze and then sponge the diluted paint onto the wall. You end up with a hint of color on top of the wall color. Adding a color wash to a room is a good way to introduce a subtle trace of color. Adding one to an image accomplishes the same thing.

You can add a color wash to a color image, but I think it's more dramatic when you apply it to a grayscale image. First you will remove the color from the image, and then you will add your color wash.

1. Open the image in Elements and make it a grayscale image (choose Image | Mode | Grayscale and click OK).

2. Change the image type to RGB color (Image | Mode | RGB Color).

3. Create a new layer in the image and make sure you are on that layer when you add the color wash.

4. Click the Foreground Color box and choose the color you want to use in the color wash.

5. Click the Paintbrush tool and select a spatter brush from the palette of brush types.

6. Click in the image area to apply the paint effect to a spot in the image.

7. Click somewhere else in the image and hold the mouse button down a little longer than usual. Notice how the paint spot darkens as you hold the button down.

8. Repeat Steps 6 and 7 until you have applied color to almost every portion of the image.

9. Reduce the opacity of the color wash layer to 50% or lower until the color you have added is a hint and not the first thing you notice about the image.

In the example image for this technique (see Figure 8-7), I reduced the opacity of the color wash layer to 50% to make sure the color wash would be obvious when it was printed in the book. You will probably want to use a much more subtle setting of 20% or lower when you color-wash your own images.

FIGURE 8-7   I used a large spatter brush to color-wash this image

You can color-wash over solid colors and fills, too. It works the same way it does when a master decorator does it in your home. Just as you would base-coat a wall with one color and then do the color wash over the top using another color, you can wash one color over another in Elements.

Did you know?

To change brush size or type while in the middle of a paint job, all you have to do is right-click. The Brush palette will open right where you clicked, and you can click another brush to switch over to it. This is OPTION-click on the Macintosh.

Flood an Image with Color

This technique is similar to that of color-washing an image, but this one applies an even color tint to the entire image at one time. Think rose-colored glasses and you've got the idea. I like using this kind of technique when I want to quickly add some subtle color to an entire image. As with the technique I just outlined, this procedure works with color images but is most effective when you layer a color over a grayscale image.

1. Open the image in Elements and make it a grayscale image.

2. Change the grayscale image into an RGB color image.

3. Add a new layer to the image and make sure you are on the new layer when you paint the image with color during the next few steps.

4. Click the Foreground Color box and select your paint color.

5. Click the Paintbrush tool to select it and click anywhere in the image area.

6. Elements fills the image area with your color. It looks as though the image has disappeared, but it's underneath the color.

7. Open the Layers window and change the opacity of the paint layer to 50% or less. The lower the setting, the more subtle the color accent.

Color-Coordinate Two Images

An all-black wardrobe is chic, but it gets boring after a while. So, even the most artistic among us need to splurge once in a while and mix a bold color accessory into their daily dose of black. The rest of us coordinate color on a daily basis when we get ready to go out into the world each day—or we should!

Coordinating the color in your wardrobe helps you look as if you have your act together and lets you mix and match clothes. Color-coordinating images does the same thing. So, if you are going to use two or more images on one page or on one poster, experiment with color-coordinating your images by following the procedure outlined here:

1. Open in Elements the two images that you want to color-coordinate. Size and arrange the windows so that you can see the two images (Image 1 and Image 2) side by side.

2. Click the Eyedropper tool and click a color in Image 1 that you want to use in Image 2. Notice that the Foreground Color box changes to the color you selected with the Eyedropper.

3. Click the Paint Bucket tool to select it. When you move the cursor into Image 2, notice the cursor looks like the Paint Bucket.

4. Click the portion of Image 2 that you want to paint with the selected color.

5. Repeat Steps 2–4 with a new color from the original image.

6. Repeat Steps 2–4, but use a color from Image 2 that is not in Image 1 and paint part of Image 1 with that color.

7. Save the two newly coordinated images with new names so that you can reuse the original images later if you want to.

When you experiment with this technique, remember that you can undo the last bucketful of paint you put in an image by choosing Undo from the Edit menu. If you want to step back even further in time, choose Step Backward from the Edit menu until you have undone all the buckets of paint that you want to remove.

I have shown you (see Figure 8-8) how to coordinate two images. You could open several onscreen at one time and move back and forth between images, using the Eyedropper to select colors and the Paint Bucket to paint them. You could use the Paintbrush, Airbrush, or Pencil to apply the colors instead of (or in addition to!) the Paint Bucket.

Make Monet Proud

When I was in college and took an art history class, I amused my professor by announcing that Monet must have been nearsighted and that's what caused him to paint such fuzzy-looking pictures. Being extremely nearsighted myself, I can relate to seeing the world in a blurry way.

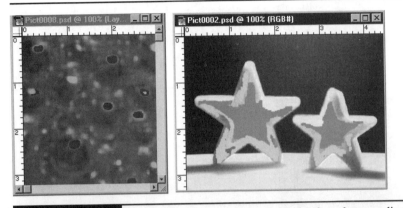

FIGURE 8-8   The two images are now completely color-coordinated

I don't know if Monet or any of the other Impressionist painters were nearsighted, but they did turn out some beautiful pictures. It took them years to perfect their artistic technique, but you can mimic it in minutes using the Impressionist Brush and a few other tools in Elements.

1. Open the image in Elements and click the Impressionist Brush tool.

2. Choose a small, hard, round brush and click around the edges of an object in your image. Notice how the area where you click starts to get blurry.

3. Switch to a larger, soft, round brush and click in the background behind the objects. Notice that the longer you hold the mouse button down, the more blurred the spot becomes.

4. Switch brush sizes and types a few times and click the foreground objects until most of the sharp edges are blurred.

5. Click the Eyedropper tool and click one of the colors in the blurry areas of the image.

6. Click the Paintbrush tool to select it and use the color in the background of the image to obscure the image details.

7. Switch back to the Impressionist Brush, select a small round brush, and blur the areas you have just painted.

8. Click the Smudge tool and smudge a few areas of the image, especially where two colors meet.

I used a simple image with easily recognizable objects in it to create my example image for this procedure (see Figure 8-9). You can use more detailed objects, but don't blur all the edges. If you do, you will end up with a colored blob that no one can recognize.

FIGURE 8-9   Dual stars done in the Impressionist style are an artistic change from the original, sharp-edged image

Craft a Color Sketch

I can't draw. If I had to illustrate by hand to make a living in the graphic arts, I would be out of a job quickly. That's why I like programs like Elements that let you take a photograph and turn it into an image that looks as if you spent hours meticulously sketching. If you can't draw, or even if you can, this is a fun technique to use to change the look of a color image.

I have used the Artistic filter called Plastic Wrap in the early part of this procedure because I wanted to create an example image that would show up well in grayscale. You could use any of the other Artistic filters and get a similar final effect. Each filter has its own unique look, though, so experiment with a few to see the differences.

1. Open the image in Elements and choose Artistic from the Filter menu. Choose Plastic Wrap from the list that appears.

2. Use the Eyedropper tool to select a prominent color from one of the objects in the foreground of the image.

3. Click the Airbrush tool and choose a soft or spatter brush. Add some color strokes to the objects in the image, the same way you might use a color highlighter to mark a line of text.

4. Change to a new color by selecting another color in the image using the Eyedropper tool. Repeat Step 3 using the Paintbrush tool.

5. Choose Brush Strokes from the Filter menu. Choose Ink Outlines from the list of filters that appears. Elements applies the filter to the image. Your image looks hand-sketched (see Figure 8-10).

FIGURE 8-10   Can you draw something like this? I can't

8

Add the Finishing Touch

A beautiful color image needs a finishing touch that is equally stunning, and too many times people use images without doing anything to set them off from the text that surrounds them. You need to add a finishing touch to images so that the images don't get overlooked in the next newsletter or annual report. Even a picture you send to your old college buddies needs a little something.

Elements allows you to quickly frame any image, but I am going to show you how to combine a few of the processes available in Elements to take your images one step beyond the ordinary.

Frame Your Picture

You have several options for framing a picture in Elements using the Frame Effects.

You can use any of the effects pictured in the frame gallery; I have chosen the Brushed Aluminum frame.

1. Open the image you want to frame in Elements.

2. Open the Effects Browser by clicking the Effects tab in the well or selecting
    Show Effects Browser from the Window menu. Elements opens the Effects
    Browser (see the next illustration).

3. Click the down-pointing triangle next to the box on the top left of the Browser
    and select Frames from the drop-down list that appears. Elements redisplays
    the Browser with just the Frame Effects.

4. Scroll through the available framing options. When you have found the one
    you want to use, click it to select it and click Apply. Elements applies the
    frame to the image.

5. A dialog box opens with the question, "Do you want to keep this Effect?"
    Click Yes to keep the effect; click No to discard it so that you can try another.

Coordinating Border

Sometimes you don't need to frame a picture—you may want to just add a touch of
texture or color around the image. That's when a coordinating border comes in handy.
Here's how to create one:

1. Open the image in Elements that you want to put the border around and check
    the image dimensions (Image | Resize | Image Size).

2. Create a new file that is the same dimensions of your image with a half inch around the edges for the boarder. Thus, to give 4″ × 5″ image a border, make the new file 5″ × 6″ in size. Make sure the new file has a transparent background.

3. Create a new layer in your blank image.

4. Use the Rectangular Lasso tool to select the whole image and copy and paste your image into the new, empty image. Center the copied image in the blank space.

5. Close the original image without saving any changes.

6. Switch to Layer 1 in the image that you have created with your copied image.

7. Use the Eyedropper tool to select a color in the image.

8. Click the Paint Bucket tool and click in the background area surrounding the copied image. Elements fills the area with your selected color.

You can create a border for your image using one of the custom fill patterns in almost the same way as you create the coordinating border. Instead of selecting a color with the Eyedropper, select a fill (Edit | Fill). The Paint Bucket tool works just the same way with a fill as with a color.

Bevel Your Image

I applied a Bevel effect to the example image (see Figure 8-11) after I added the border. I wanted to make the image stand out more against the border. Since I did it, I want to show you how it's done so that you can do it, too:

1. After creating the border, choose Layer Styles from the well or select Show Layer Styles from the Window menu.

2. The Layer Styles browser appears. If Bevels is not shown in the box in the upper left-hand corner of the Browser, click the down-pointing triangle next to the box and select Bevels from the drop-down list that appears.

3. Click one of the layer styles to select it and Elements applies it to the image. It does not apply it to the border, since the program sees the border as a layer of color and not an image.

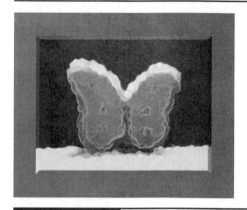

FIGURE 8-11   I used a bevel on this image to set it apart from the border

Create a Fabric Frame

I saw a project like this in a craft magazine not too long ago, only, as you can imagine, they used real fabric to create a frame. We're going to use fabric we create out of the various fills in Elements, plus some parts of the image itself. This is a really fun project to do whether you do it with real fabric or fabric you spin up inside of Elements.

1. Open the image in Elements that you want to put the border around and check the image dimensions (Image | Resize | Image Size).

2. Create a new file that is the same dimensions of your image with a half inch around the edges for the border. Thus, to give 4″ × 5″ image a border, make the new file 5″ × 6″ in size. Make sure the new file has a transparent background.

3. Create a new layer in your blank image.

4. Use the Rectangular Lasso tool to select the whole image and copy and paste your image into the new, empty image. Center the copied image in the blank space.

5. Close the original image without saving any changes.

6. Switch to Layer 1 in the image that you have created with your copied image.

7. Use the Rectangle tool to draw a small rectangle in the upper-left portion of the border area.

8. Select a Custom Fill (Edit | Fill) to be your first fabric swatch.

9. Draw another rectangle beneath the first and fill it with a color that's in the image.

10. Repeat Steps 8 and 9 until the entire border of the image is surrounded by rectangles, alternating a fill with a solid color. Once you have two or more custom fills around the image, you can fill some of the solid color rectangles with a color in one of the custom fills.

11. Resize some of the rectangles so that they are shorter than some of the others. Make sure the entire border area is covered with your "fabric pieces."

12. Select one of the fabric pieces and apply one of the Texture filters to it (Filter | Texture). It doesn't matter which one—in fact, it's fun to start at the top of the list of filters, use one at a time, and then start over at the top if you need to.

The fabric frame for my sample image took some time to create (see Figure 8-12). I experimented with various fills and filters for the fabric pieces. Still, this was the last image in this chapter, so I wanted it to look great. I hope you like it.

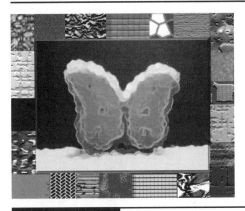

FIGURE 8-12   Here's my fabric frame, created with fills and colors and finished off with a few Texture filters

Summary

Color, correctly chosen and properly applied, can make all the difference in an image. In Elements you have many of the same color correction tools that professional graphic artists use. They are powerful tools, and you can learn to use them to make your images attract more attention or look better than you ever thought possible. Now that you've seen some of the color tools in action, it's time to move on and show you another way to change an image's appearance—by using filters.

How to…

■ Apply a filter

■ Change filter settings

■ Twirl and blend colors in an image

■ Liquify an image

■ Apply filters to different parts of the same image

■ Use fabric and filters to create a background

■ Use filters to make variations of one image

■ Create a custom filter

In earlier chapters, I have used filters a few times, but this chapter is a systematic look at filters. While I don't show you every filter and every setting even in this chapter, I show you many of the filters here. If I were to show you all the filters in their almost infinite variety and combinations, it would take an entire book.

I want to show you what some of the filters can do and then show you some of the images you can create using the filters. So in a way, this chapter is a reference guide and a collection of recipes for using filters to change images. Look through the material in the chapter, and if you see an image that catches your eye, try the procedure that I used to create it. Experiment with the filters and their settings. Make sure to write down the filters and the settings that result in the images you like best, and then create your own filter recipes.

I have included a filter gallery in the color section of this book because most of the filters look best when applied to color images.

Easy One-Filter Changes

One filter can do a lot to change an image, which is why I start this section out with about a dozen examples of what one filter can do to the same image. Figure 9-1 is the "before" image. I will walk you through the settings for the filter, if there are any settings, that I used to create the image, but since many of the filter windows look alike, I won't show you every filter settings window.

| FIGURE 9-1 | This is the "before" image |

Make an Image Look Like a Watercolor

1.   Open the image in Elements.

2.   Select Artistic from the Filter menu.

3.   Choose Watercolor from the list that appears. The Watercolor controls window appears and you see a preview in the window, as shown next. The higher the settings are in this filter, the more obvious and heavy the results are, so keep the settings under 10.

4.   Click OK and Elements applies the filter effect.

As you can see from the "after" image for this filter (see Figure 9-2), the Watercolor filter can give an image a homespun look. I like to use this filter on images that I like to imagine could have been watercolor pictures to begin with.

FIGURE 9-2   If you like watercolor images, try the Watercolor filter

Blur an Image

When you blur an image, you push the visual effect of the image way down, so it fades into the back of the mind of the person viewing the image. They hardly notice it. So, if you want to use the shapes in an image but don't want people to notice the details, blurring an image is a good way to do that.

1. Open the image in Elements and select Blur from the Filter menu.

2. Select Blur More from the list of filters that appears.

3. Elements applies the effect, and you see the image is a little blurry.

4. Repeat Step 2 until you get the amount of blurring you want the image to have.

To get my after image (see Figure 9-3), I had to use the Blur More filter ten times. I wanted to make sure the change was really obvious to you.

FIGURE 9-3	When you use the Blur filter, try it several times in a row to see a pronounced blurring on the image

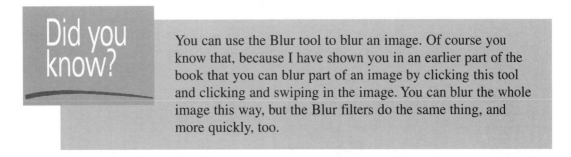

Did you know?

You can use the Blur tool to blur an image. Of course you know that, because I have shown you in an earlier part of the book that you can blur part of an image by clicking this tool and clicking and swiping in the image. You can blur the whole image this way, but the Blur filters do the same thing, and more quickly, too.

Enhance the Blur

You may have wondered if there was a faster way to blur an image, and the answer is most definitely yes. Nothing fuzzy about the way Elements lets you blur images quickly. Here's one of the ways you can blur an image and control the amount of blur that is applied.

1. Open the image in Elements and choose Blur from the Filter menu.

2. Choose Gaussian Blur from the list of filters that appears. If Elements asks if you want to simplify a layer before you continue, click OK.

3. The Gaussian Blur control window appears. Type **10** in the Radius box. The maximum setting for the radius is 250, but if you get much beyond 50, the image could be too blurry. Experiment and see which setting you like best; the best setting might vary from image to image.

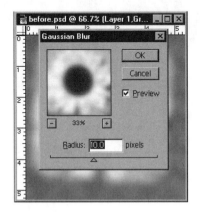

4. Click OK and Elements applies the filter to the image.

As promised, the Gaussian blur filter obscures the features of an image, leaving you with an object that is not easily recognizable. You wouldn't know my after image (see Figure 9-4) is a sunflower without seeing the before image.

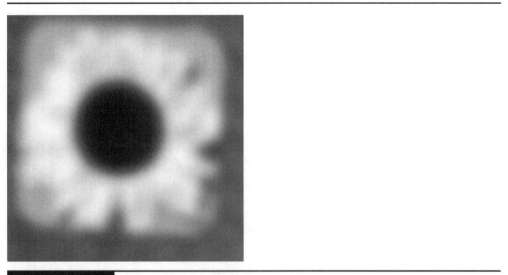

FIGURE 9-4   Here is the sunflower after I applied the Gaussian Blur filter

Extrude an Image

This is an interesting filter that makes an image looks as though you chopped it to pieces or made tiny pyramids out of it. I wouldn't use this filter with every image, so I suggest you try it with a few different ones to get a feel for the kinds of images you might like to use the filter with. I want to show you the filter because it's unusual and easy.

I also want to show you a different way to choose a filter using the menu-based procedure. The way I am going to use for this procedure and the next is a good way to go shopping for a filter. Plus, it's easy to change from one filter to another this way, allowing you to shop for hours if you let yourself.

1. Open the image in Elements and click the Filters tab on the palette well.

2. The Filter palette opens. Make sure "All" is the word showing in the box at the upper left-hand side of the box, shown as follows:

3. If "All" is not showing, click the down triangle and select All from the list.

4. Scroll through the thumbnail examples of the filters and click Extrude.

5. Drag the thumbnail onto the image. The Extrude window opens.

6. Select Pyramids and set the size of pixels to 50 by typing in **50** in the box.

7. Type **75** in the Depth box and select Random.

8. Click OK and Elements applies the filter.

The after image is looking rather pointed, isn't it (see Figure 9-5)? That's because I used the Pyramids setting. If you want something less pointed, choose Blocks instead of Pyramids.

FIGURE 9-5   Want pyramids in your image? Try the Extrude filter

Crosshatch an Image

This is an interesting filter to me because it makes an image look as though drawn with diagonal strokes. I would use this filter with images that have a lot of obvious lines or lots of color—I think the filter would bring out the artistic best in these kinds of images.

1. Open the image in Elements and click the Filters tab.

2. Scroll down through the thumbnails and click Crosshatch.

3. The Crosshatch controls window opens.

4. Slide the controls for each setting until they are in the middle of each slider.

5. Click OK and Elements applies the filter.

Notice how, in my after image (see Figure 9-6), the filter has changed the frame around the flower into crosshatches. The filter also put some crosshatches in the flower, but you can see the filter effect in the border much more.

Welcome to the color insert section of this book—I will show you how wonderful you can make your images look by using the techniques outlined in the rest of the book. First, I will show you how to take an old photograph and make it look better. Then I will show you what some of the filters look like when applied to a photograph. After that, I will show you how some of the special features look. Finally, you will see samples of color fills, text, and bevel style examples, and examples of images with more than one filter applied.

Fix an Old Photograph

This is a photograph of me when I was four years old. My mother made me and my sister matching Easter dresses.

I color balanced and color corrected the photo. It looks much better now.

I fixed the scratches and colored over some of the stains on the image. I also cut it using an oval selection marquee with a feathered edge. I didn't want the image to look brand new, so I stopped here.

Filter Gallery

Elements has so many filters, filter controls, and filter combinations that it would take a whole book to show you all the possible combinations. I took the original image you see below and applied different filters.

This is the original image—a shot of an iron bridge I took in a nearby park last fall.

Artistic/Colored Pencil

Artistic/Palette Knife

Brush Strokes/Dark Strokes

Distort/Displace Glass

Pixelate/Pointillize

Sketch/Halftone Pattern

Stylize/Extrude

Stylize/Glowing Edges

Texture/Craquelure

Texture/Stained Glass

Seven filters in one image, left to right: Texture/Stained Glass, Artistic/Neon Glow, Distort/Wave, Pizelate/Mezzotint, Sketch/Water Paper, Stylize/Tiles, Texture/Grain

Special Effects Gallery

Elements has many special effects that you can use to change the look of an image in one step.

Original Image

Neon Nights

Blizzard

Colorful Center

Fluorescent Chalk

Marbled Glass

Special Effect Looks and Frames

Elements has special effects that work like fills. Here are a few of these effects, along with some special effects frames.

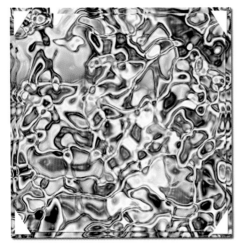

Green Slime with
Photo Corners

Gold Sprinkles with
Ripple Frame

Sunset with Waves
Frame

Wood-Rosewood with
Wood Frame

Rusted Metal with
Wild Frame

Sandpaper with Brushed
Aluminum Frame

Color Fills

You can fill any object in Elements with a custom fill. Here are some custom fills that are available to you.

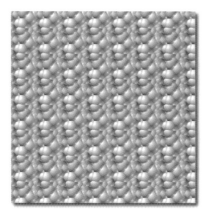

Bubbles

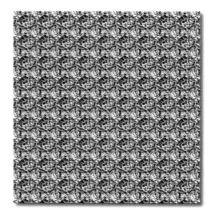

Nebula

Satin

Woven

Wood

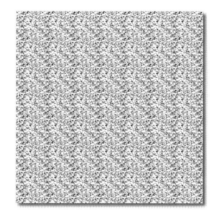

Wrinkles

Optical Checkerboard

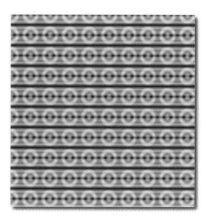

Tie Dye

Text Effects and Bevels in Action

I love the special looks you can get with text effects in Elements. I added some bevels so you can see what a difference they make in an image.

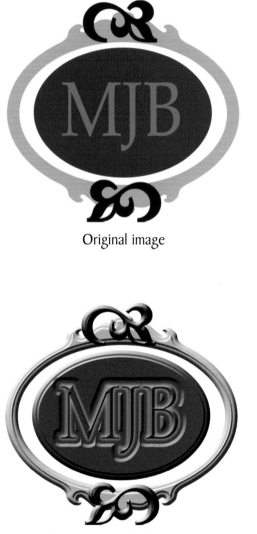

Original image

Brushed Metal/Simple Emboss and Simple Outer Bevel on the text and all other objects

Inner Ridge on text, Scalloped Oval on everything else

Wood Paneling/Simple Pillow on text, Emboss on all portions, and Inner Ridge on the oval

Multiple Filter Effects

Here are two examples of the results you can acheive when you combine filters. I added text to the original image, and in some cases applied multiple filters to the background only of the image.

Here's the original. Notice the text I added to the image.

I used the Pixelate/Crystallize filter and then the Texture/Texturizer filters.

Here's the original. I added some text to the photograph and gave the text layer 52% opacity.

I used the Distort/Diffuse Glow filter, then the Blur/Motion Blur, Stylize/Wind, and finally the Artistic/Colored Pencil filters on the background of the original image.

FIGURE 9-6   You can see the crosshatch filter effect much more in the border of the image than in the flower area

NOTE   *If you click the Apply button on the Filters palette after you click a thumbnail of a filter, Elements opens the settings window for that filter (if there are any settings that can be changed).*

9

Warp an Image

Did you ever feel like really shaking up a standard idea just to see what the result would be? The Liquify filter turns an image into digital finger paint. Just as you can drag your fingertip through a painting that isn't quite dry and alter the appearance of the image, you can do the same when you use the Liquify filter (see Figures 9-7 and 9-8).

1. Open the image in Elements and choose Liquify from the Filter menu. The Liquify window opens.

2. Set the brush size at 50 by typing **50** in the Brush Size box.

3. Set the brush pressure at 50 by typing **50** in the Brush Pressure box.

4. Click anywhere in the image, hold down the mouse button, and swirl left and right.

5. Repeat Step 4 a few times until the image is a swirl of color.

6. Push one color into another by clicking the first color and pushing it into another color. Notice how the colors blend when you do this.

FIGURE 9-7   This is our starting point—we're going to swirl and warp this image

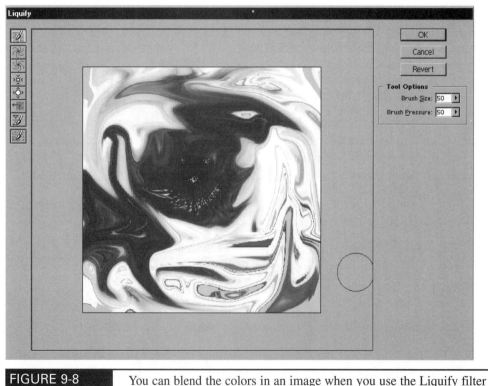

FIGURE 9-8   You can blend the colors in an image when you use the Liquify filter

Marbleize an Image

Now that you know how to swirl an image using the Liquify filter, let me show you a variation on the same idea that lets you do something I bet you never knew you could do (unless you are a stonecutter). In this procedure, I want to show you how to make an image look like marble, and then show you how to create a marble tile pattern to use in other images or as background for other objects.

You can also create your own custom-color marble by using the next procedure. Use a grayscale image if you only want shades of gray in your marble; use a brightly colored image if you want marble with many colors. If you use another image, skip the first five steps and pick up with Step 6 after opening your image in Elements.

1. Create a new file in Elements.

2. Draw a rectangle in the image area and fill it with the color you want your marble to be.

3. Use the Paintbrush to paint diagonal lines across the rectangle. Use one of the other colors you want to be seen in your slab of marble.

4. Switch to a larger or smaller brush and a different brush type and paint a few more lines.

5. Repeat Steps 3 and 4 with another color and other brush sizes and types. The following illustration is the image after I have drawn some diagonal lines:

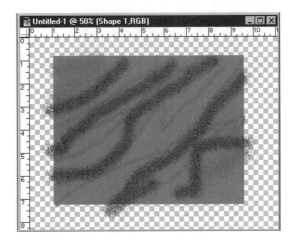

6. Open the Liquify window (Filter | Liquify).

7. Click the Shift Pixels tool, which is the sixth icon on the toolbar on the left of the window.

8. Set the brush size at 25 and the brush pressure at 50.

9. Following your diagonal lines, stroke diagonally through the image.

10. Stroke through the image in the other diagonal direction several times so that your diagonal strokes cross each other.

11. Change the brush size to 15 and the brush pressure to 75.

12. Repeat Steps 9 and 10.

I really like this procedure because, as you can see from my finished image (see Figure 9-9), it's easy to create and you can get some profoundly attractive-looking marble slabs with it in a short period of time.

FIGURE 9-9   You can create a marble slab like this in less than ten minutes

Create a Marble Background

Once you have created a slab of marble, you can trim it down into smaller pieces and use the marble tiles to construct a marble background.

1. Open the file that contains your marble slab in Elements.

2. Create a new file for your background and object.

3. Click the Rectangular Marquee tool and select Fixed Size from the Style menu (click the down arrow next to the Style box and select Fixed Size from the list that appears).

4. Type in **2 in** for the width and height of your tile in the Width and Height boxes. If you find these dimensions are too small for your desired tile size, use larger ones.

5. Click anywhere in the image and Elements opens a rectangular marquee where you clicked.

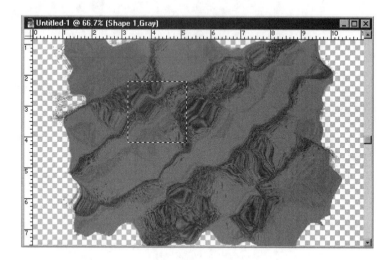

6. Copy and paste the tile into your new image (Edit | Copy, switch to the other file, Edit | Paste).

7. Repeat Steps 5 and 6 using different areas of the marble slab until you have enough tiles to create your background.

8. Move the tiles around so that they butt against each other.

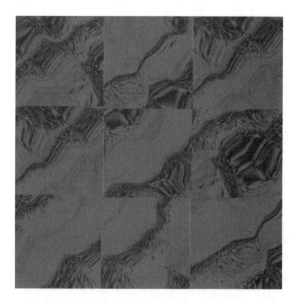

NOTE *Here are some other ways you can set these tiles that will give you distinctly different looks with only a little more effort: You can leave a little space between them and fill the background behind the tiles with a color selected from one of the tiles—instant grout lines! Or, you can rotate the marble tiles before you set them in place (click the tile, select Flip Horizontal or Flip Vertical from the Image menu).*

Change Part of an Image, Part 1

As promised, I will show you how to apply a filter (or any change) to only part of an image. In this, part one of two parts, I will show you how to select a portion of an image and apply one filter. In the second part of this procedure, I will show you how to select another part of the image and apply a different filter to that part of the image.

The first part of this procedure is to tell Elements what part of the image to change. Then you can apply the filter or make the change to that part of the image only.

1. Click the Magic Wand tool and type **100** in the Tolerance box. The lower the Tolerance setting, the closer the colors have to be to the color where you clicked in order to be selected. The higher the number, the greater the color variety can be.

2. Click anywhere in the area you want to select. Elements will select a portion of the area around where you click based on the color similarities in the surrounding area.

9

3. Adjust the selected area if necessary; click the appropriate button on the controls for the tool and click in the area. For example, to select more of the image, click the Add To Selection button. To reduce the selection area, click the Subtract From Selection button.

4. Apply the filter to the selected area. I used the Emboss filter (Stylize | Emboss) on my sample image.

When you emboss an image, you give it a feeling of depth similar to what an embossing tool does with a piece of paper. In my finished image (see Figure 8-10), you can see that the center of the sunflower has been embossed.

FIGURE 9-10   I embossed the center of the sunflower

Change Part of an Image, Part 2

In the last procedure I showed you how to apply a filter to one part of an image. In this procedure, I will show you how to apply another filter to the rest of the image. If you saved the image from the last procedure, open it in Elements. In the steps, I assume you have not closed the image.

1. If the portion of the image you selected earlier is still selected, deselect it (Select | Deselect).

2. Make sure the Magic Wand tool is selected. Click the part of the image that has not been changed.

3. Adjust the selection area, if necessary. I used 50 instead of 100 for the Tolerance setting to get just the petals of the sunflower and not the background as well.

4. Apply the filter to this newly selected area. I used the Brush Strokes/Ink Outlines filter for the sunflower petals in the following example image:

9

Fashion a Brass Button

In this procedure, I will show you how to take a simple round image and turn it into a brass button. Once you have created such an image, you can use it to accessorize almost any other image, or you could use it as button on a Web page.

1. Create a new image in Elements that is five inches square and has a transparent background.

2. Use the Ellipse drawing tool and draw a circle that almost fills the image area.

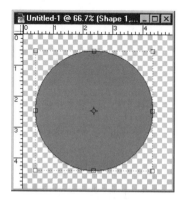

3. Use the Paint Bucket to fill the circle with a shade of orange/red.

4. Draw a smaller circle inside the first one and fill it with a darker shade of the orange/red color.

5. Simplify the layer the smaller circle is on (Layer | Simplify Layer) so that you can draw on that layer.

6. Draw four smaller circles, fill them with black, and arrange them in the center of the button (buttonholes!).

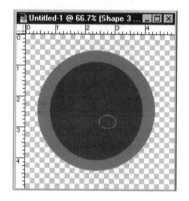

7. Click the outer circle. Apply the Scalloped Edge Bevel to it (Open the Layer Styles palette and select Bevels from the drop-down list, then select the Scalloped Edge Bevel).

8. Click the inner circle and apply the Inner Ridge Bevel to it.

9. Apply the Simple Shape Pillow Emboss Bevel to each buttonhole.

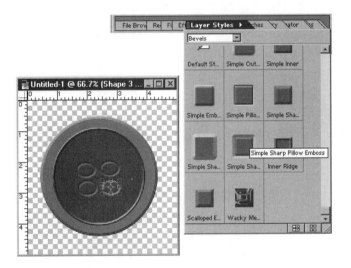

9

10. Click the outer circle and apply the Add Noise filter (Noise | Add Noise). Doing this adds a brushed metal look to the outer circle of the button.

Rain on Your Image

You know how you can look out through a window on a really rainy day and
see the world through the raindrops? What if you could add that romantic, misty
look to any image? Well, you can by using the right filter. Here's how to rain on
any image:

1. Open the image in Elements and click the Smudge tool.

2. Select one of the spatter brushes. Set the pressure of the brush at 50 percent or
   higher.

3. Start at the top of the image and drag down vertically several times (raindrops
   run down the glass pane, don't they?). Make sure all your strokes don't start at
   the top of the image.

4. Change the brush to another size of spatter brush and increase or decrease the
   brush pressure. Add several more strokes.

5. Select Pixelate from the Filter menu. Select Crystallize from the list of filters
   that appears.

6. Set the Cell Size at 10 or lower, as you can see in the next illustration.
   Anything higher and the image will look like it's made up of large pieces
   of glass.

What you get when you finish is a very dreamy image, even if what you started out with was not too exciting. As you can see from the finished image (see Figure 9-11), adding the streaks to the image before you used the filter helped add the idea of rain running down the glass pane.

FIGURE 9-11   This is a romantic, dreamy image, and it was all done in a few steps

Use More Than One Filter

I have shown you how to use one filter on one image and two different filters on one image. Now I want to show you some of the effects you can get when you use more than one filter on an image. We'll start with the before image shown in Figure 9-12, and I'll walk you through a few procedures that use two or more filters.

FIGURE 9-12   This is the before image—notice the large leaves in the picture

Flood an Image with Light

1. Open the image in Elements and select Artistic from the Filter menu.

2. Select Underpainting from the list of filters that appears.

3. Change the controls for the filter to: Brush Size 5, Texture Coverage 25, Texture Burlap, Scaling 50%, Relief 0, and Light Direction Left, as shown here:

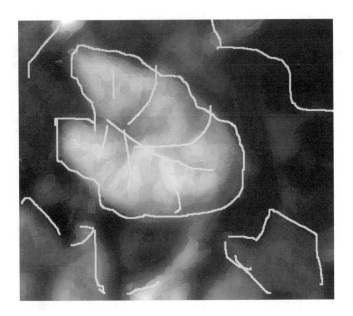

4. Click the Pencil tool and trace some of the edges in the image. Use a light color or white to make sure the lines stand out.

9

5. Click the Impressionist Brush and blur some of the lines you've drawn.

6. Select the Chalk and Charcoal filter from the Sketch group of filters (Filter | Sketch | Chalk and Charcoal). Put all the settings on "5."

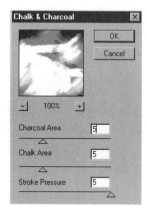

7. Click the Smudge tool and blur some of the parts of the image that aren't needed, as I did—you can see the effect in the following after image. I wanted the leaf shape to stand out, so I blurred a little of the area around the leaf.

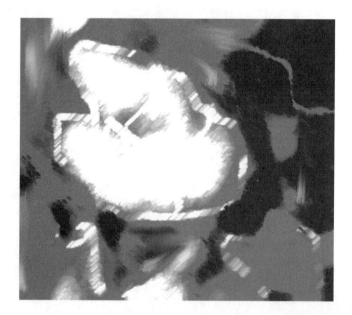

Turn Fabric into a Background

A background fills the screen with its presence, and it is good to have a lot of different backgrounds in your collection of images. Unfortunately, it can be difficult to come up with lots of different looks. Here's one way to create a unique background: First, grab a piece of patterned fabric and your camera and take a picture of the cloth. Then, either scan the image or, if you used your digital camera, use the image you took with the camera. You can also scan the fabric itself by laying the cloth flat on the scanner glass.

As you can see from the before image (see Figure 9-13), I used an old bandanna.

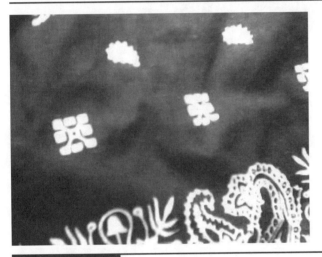

FIGURE 9-13   Here's the before image—part of a bandanna

9

1. Open the image in Elements.

2. Click the Dodge tool and click somewhere in the image. Use the Dodge tool to fade some of the color in the fabric.

3. Click the Rectangular Marquee and select a portion of the image.

4. Select Stylize from the Filter menu.

5. Select Solarize from the list of filters that appears. Elements applies this filter to the area you selected, as shown here:

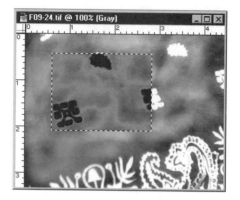

6. Repeat Steps 3–5.

7. Select Blur from the Filter menu. Select Motion Blur from the list of filters. The Motion Blur window appears.

8. Set the Angle at 0 and the Distance at 10, as shown here:

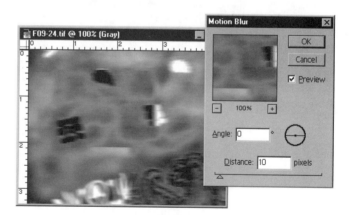

9. Click OK and Elements blurs the image.

10. Select Adjustments from the Image menu. Select Invert from the list that appears.

When you create a background, you want to include some objects that are visually interesting, which patterned fabric usually is. However, if you use fabric as your starting point, you want to keep the visual interest but make it much less obvious what you started with. You don't want people to wonder why you have fabric on your Web page! That's why I blurred the image and then inverted it. As you can see in Figure 9-14, the final image is interesting, but unless you knew we started with some fabric, you wouldn't know for sure what the image is.

FIGURE 9-14   This is the final image after all the changes—it would be a good background image

Create Variations on Images

I like the idea of taking a simple image and using the filters in Elements to make several variations of the image. I like to use those images in a single large image, such as a poster, to help bracket more important objects in the poster. Or, I use these images side-by-side to create an artistic-looking image. Here's how to take one image and, by using different filter combinations, make several variations of that image.

My before image (see Figure 9-15) is a close-up shot of, believe it or not, a ball made of small twigs wound around each other.

1. Open the image in Elements and apply the Artistic | Accented Edges filter twice. It doesn't matter what the settings for the filter are. Experiment if you like, but use the same settings twice.

2. Apply a Neon Glow (Artistic | Neon Glow) to the image. Use any glow size or glow brightness settings you would like, but use a bright blue color.

3. Save the image with a new name.

4. Apply the same filter again with the same settings but use a different, equally bright color.

5. Save the file with a different name.

FIGURE 9-15   The before image is made up of lots of small twigs

6. Repeat Steps 4 and 5 as many times as you need to in order to create the number of files you need. Use a different bright color each time. Figure 9-16 is an example of what you can do.

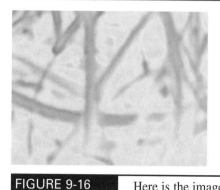

FIGURE 9-16   Here is the image after I have applied the Neon Glow filter

Create Your Own Filter

You can create your own filter in Elements, and after you have created it, you can use it just as you would any of the ready-made filters. Here's how to create and save your own filter.

1. Open an image in Elements.

2. Open the Filters palette and click Custom.

3. Drag the Custom thumbnail over the image and the Custom settings window opens, as shown here:

4. Change the numbers in the boxes until you like the new filter you have created.

5. Click Save and the Save window opens.

6. Give the filter a name by typing the name in the File Name box.

7. Click Save to save the new filter. The Save window closes.

8. Click OK on the Custom window to apply the filter. Elements applies the filter and closes the Custom window.

Figure 9-17 is the after image of the sunflower with my custom-made filter. It's kind of an industrial-strength embossing filter. I like it.

Load a Custom Filter

Once you've created the filter, you will want to use it again and again. Here's how you load and use a custom filter:

1. Open the image in Elements and open the Filters palette.

2. Drag the Custom thumbnail over the image. The Custom window appears.

3. Click Load, and the Load window opens. Click the name of the custom filter you want to use.

4. Click the Load button. The Load window closes.

5. Click OK in the Custom window. Elements applies the filter and closes the Custom window.

FIGURE 9-17   This is the sunflower image after I applied my custom filter to it

Summary

When you work with filters in Elements, the main limits on what you can do are set by your imagination and by the time you have available—not the technology. That's good, in a way, because the more you work with filters, the more productive your imagination and your time spent using them become. You do need to practice using filters and experiment with them to get the most of out them. I hope this chapter helps you get started doing just that.

Part IV

Add Text Elements to Your Images

Chapter 10

Add and Edit Text

How to…

- Add horizontal text to an image
- Change the appearance of text
- Place text along a curve
- Remove text from an image
- Apply text effects

So far I have shown you many of the ways you can change images using the tools and capabilities in Elements. We haven't talked a lot about text in images, but that's not because you can't do a lot with text in Elements. In fact, you can do so much with text in the program that I needed two chapters to tell you everything.

Chapter 10 is the first of the two chapters related to text; in this chapter, I cover the basics of adding and changing text within an image. In Chapter 11, I'll show you how to take the basics and move up a notch or two in design terms. Not only do we create and edit text in that chapter, but also we create some really cool-looking images.

Before we dive into the projects in this chapter, though, I want to talk about some of the terms and concepts that apply to text in Elements. The first is "point," which is a term printers coined centuries ago as a unit of measure for a letter. They needed something to measure type with, since type usually isn't inches high! The measuring system used for type is related to inches; a point is $\frac{1}{72}$ of an inch. (Six points equals one pica, if you had seen that term and wondered what it means.) So, a 36-point size will give you a letter about half an inch high. Normally, body text (what you're reading now) is about 10- or 12-point type. Headlines are larger—say, about 36 to 72 points.

How to … Change the Letter Units

In Elements, the default system for indicating type sizes is in points, but you can change the unit of measurement if you are not familiar with points and don't wish to become familiar with the concept. Here's how to make the change: Launch Elements, but you don't have to open a file. Select Preferences from the Edit menu. Select Units & Rulers from the list that appears. The Preferences window opens. Click the down arrow next to the Type box and select either pixels or mm (millimeters) from the list that appears.

You will see the term *anti-aliased* on the Options toolbars whenever you create type in Elements. There is a check box next to the term; by default, the box has a check in it. I suggest you work with anti-aliased type all the time, so please make sure that you do not click the box and turn off anti-aliasing. Briefly, when you create text in Elements, to get a nice, smooth edge to your text rather than a jagged appearance around the edges, you need to keep the check on in this box.

One more piece of background information: The classic definition of a typeface is a collection of letters and characters in all its many varieties—normal, bold, italic, and so on. A font is a part of a typeface collection. Think of it this way: your family is composed of everyone you are related to, and your brother is part of your family. The family is the typeface, and your brother is a font!

In Elements, the two terms (typeface and font) are defined slightly differently, which can lead to confusion if you are familiar with the classic definitions. That's why I wanted to explain how Elements treats text before you start into the projects in this chapter. A typeface in Elements is a set of characters, and when you select a typeface, you select a font family and then a font style. If your computer does not have all the styles for a particular font family installed on it, some of the font style selections will not be available for that font.

Add Text to an Image

In this project, I show you how to add a few words to an image. It's a simple project, but it's enough to get us started. I will use the same image to show you how to edit text and change it as we progress through the chapter. You don't need the image I have to learn these procedures; any image will do.

1. Open the image you want to add text to in Elements. Click the Text tool. Notice the different sections on the Options bar that appears above the image, and note that the cursor has changed into an I-beam.

2. Change the point size to 24 by clicking the down arrow next to the Point Size box (the third box from the left on the Options bar) and select 24 pt from the list that appears, as shown in the following illustration. Notice the different type sizes you could choose. Or you could type in any number in the box.

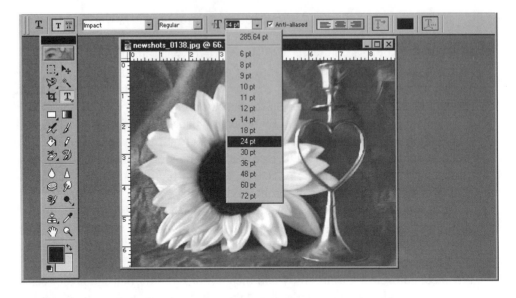

3. Type is the same color as the foreground color. So, if the foreground color isn't black, change the type color to black by clicking the Foreground Color square on the toolbox. Select black from the Color Picker window that appears by clicking an area of the square that is black. Click OK to close the window.

4. Click in the area of the image that you want to add the text to. A blinking vertical line appears where you click.

5. Type your text and your image will have text in it—as does the sample shown here.

How to ...   **Delete Text**

To get rid of a piece of text you added to an image, you can delete it after you select it. To select it, click the Move tool and then click the text to select it. Then press DELETE. Elements will open a dialog box and ask you if you wish to delete the layer with the text on it. Click Yes. The box closes, and Elements deletes the text. Another way to delete a piece of text is to click the Text tool, then select the text you want to remove and press DELETE. Whatever you select is deleted, so if you only want a portion of the piece of text to go away, select only that portion. You can also delete a text object by throwing away the layer it is on.

Change Text Formatting

In order to do this procedure, you must already have created some text in your image. Once you learn how to change the appearance of text, you can make your selections for text before you start typing.

1. Before you can edit text, you must first select the text. So, with the image from the last procedure still open in Elements, make sure the Text tool is still active. Click at the beginning of the line of text, hold the mouse button down, and slide to the right until the entire line of text is selected.

2. Change the font by clicking the down arrow next to the font family box (the first box on the Options bar). Select a typeface from the list that appears. The list that appears reflects the fonts installed on the computer you are working on; it may vary from computer to computer. Elements changes the typeface.

3. Change the type style by clicking the down arrow next to the Font Style box. Select Bold Italic from the list that appears. Elements applies the change to the type.

4. Make the type bigger by choosing 36 from the Font Size list (see instructions in the last procedure for details on how to select a point size). After you select the point size, Elements makes the type bigger, as you can see in the following image:

How to ...   Change Before Typing

The type appearance selections stay at whatever they were the last time you created some type. You can change them to different selections before you start typing so that the text looks the way you want it to from the beginning. To make this happen, after you click the Text tool, select the settings (font family, font style, etc.) before you start typing.

Move Text

The image from the last procedure looks great—except for one thing. You can't see all of the text. Part of it runs over into the darker part of the image. You can fix this problem in a couple of ways. In this procedure, I will show you how to fix it by moving the text. Later on in the chapter, I will show you some other ways to make the text more visible.

1. Click the Move tool to get out of text editing mode. Notice how small squares appear at the corners and the middle of the sides of the text area. These squares are called handles. If you don't see the handles, click the line of text.

2. Click the line of text, hold down the mouse button, and drag the text somewhere else in the image area.

3. Release the mouse button when you have the text where you want it to be.

Add Vertical Text to an Image

Earlier I showed you how to add horizontal text to an image. That's what you'll want to do most of the time—most people in Western cultures read left to right along a horizontal plane, right? Sometimes, though, you may want to add vertical text to an image—that's text that starts at the top and works its way down. Doing so adds visual interest to an image, but don't use vertical text for large text blocks. It is hard to read easily.

1. Open the image in Elements that you want to add the vertical text to. (I am going to use the image from the last procedure—see Figure 10-1.)

2. Right-click the Text tool and select Vertical Type tool from the list that appears. Notice how the Text tool appearance changes: it has a small arrow on the left that is pointing down after you do this.

3. Click in the image where you want the top of the line of text to start. Notice that the cursor changes to a horizontal blinking line.

4. Make your text appearance selections using the Options bar.

FIGURE 10-1   In keeping with the B&B theme, I added the word "pancakes" to my image

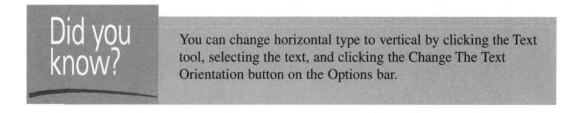

Did you know?   You can change horizontal type to vertical by clicking the Text tool, selecting the text, and clicking the Change The Text Orientation button on the Options bar.

Underline Text

Underlining is another way to draw attention to a piece of text. I am not a big fan of underlined text when the underlining goes on for more than a few words. I think underlined text is hard to read when the underlining goes on line after line; the underlining becomes a distraction. That said, it's not distracting when you underline a word or two in a short phrase—doing so can reinforce your message. Here's how to underline text in Elements:

1. Open the image in Elements and add a few words of horizontal text to the image.

2. Select the portion of the text that you want to underline. Notice how the objects on the Options bar change when you do this.

3. Click the Show Text Options button on the Options bar (this button is not on the Options bar until you select the text). The Text Options list appears.

4. Click Underline Text. Elements applies the underline to the selected text, as shown in Figure 10-2.

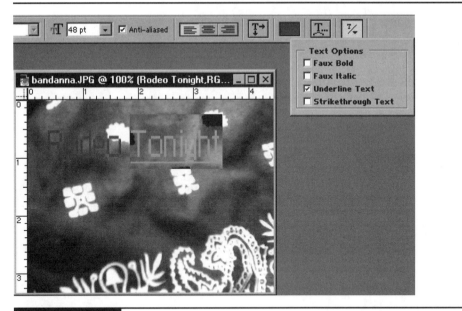

FIGURE 10-2   These are the four text options that appear when you click the Show Text Options button

How to ...   **Strike Through Text**

When you want to strike through text—that is, to put a line through the text to indicate it should be ignored or deleted, you follow the same steps as you would to underline the text, except you should choose Strikethrough Text instead of Underline Text. Using strikethrough text is a good way to draw attention to something in a backward kind of way. You might, for example, show a to-do list with several items done (shown as strikethrough text) and the item at the bottom still not done. Wouldn't that make a memorable image?

Curve Text

One of the neat things you can do with text in Elements is to curve it, and you can curve it in many different ways. In this procedure, I show you how to create a simple text curve. In the next chapter, I return to this basic procedure and use it in several projects to create more elaborate text effects.

1. Open the image in Elements and click the Text tool.

2. Create a horizontal line of text. I underlined mine to make the curve show up better, as you can see in the following illustration:

10

3. Click the Create Warped Text button on the Options bar. If when you do this you get a message that says Elements can't carry out this action because the font has no outline data, select the text and change to a different font until you get one that works.

4. The Warp Text window opens. Click the down arrow next to the Style box and choose Arc from the list that appears (see the next illustration). The list disappears and you are back at the Warp Text window.

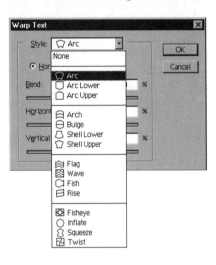

5. Click Horizontal and type **+50** in the Bend box.

6. Type **10** in the Horizontal Distortion box and **0** in the Vertical Distortion box.

7. Click OK and Elements curves the text, as shown in the next illustration.

10

How to ...   **Preview a Typeface**

To check and see what your text would look like in a different typeface without applying that typeface, select the text and highlight a font name in the font box in the horizontal toolbar. Elements will show you what the text would look like in that font; use the arrow keys to go up and down the list and get a preview of the type in action.

Remove Text from an Image

I like the fact that my camera records the date on each photograph, because having a date on the image helps me remember when I took the photo.

I don't like it, though, when I want to use the image and find the date is in a crucial part of the image. I can't crop it out, but I can hide it. That's why I wanted to show you how to remove text from an image, but you can use this technique anytime you find yourself reading something in an image that you would rather not be seeing.

1. Open the image in Elements and zoom in on the part of the image that contains the unwanted text, as I have done in my sample image shown here:

2. Click the Clone Stamp tool and select a small brush for the tool.

3. Select a part of the image that is similar to part of the image near the text area.

4. Click the part of the text that is near the area you have sampled. Work gingerly in the area, using the cloned part of the image to replace the text.

5. Repeat Steps 3 and 4 using other parts of the image to replace other parts of the text. The trick is to find a part of the image to clone that is really similar to the part that would be visible if the date had never been there. In my sample image (see the next illustration), I have cloned bits of the tree and sky to replace part of the date.

6. Change the size of your brush, zoom in more, and use the Clone tool to eliminate the last fragments of the text.

7. Zoom out so that you can check your work from where people will view the finished image. In my sample figure at the normal view zoom level, the date is no longer visible.

8. Repeat Step 6 if there are any tiny parts of the text still visible at the normal viewing size for the image.

Create a Stencil Effect

Now that I've shown you the basics of creating and editing text, let me close out this chapter with a few simple projects that use the text effects built into Elements. Text effects are an easy and fast (really fast) way to change the look of a piece of text. I like them so much I have put together a gallery of text effects in the color section of the book so that you can see what they are like.

In this procedure, I want to show you how to use one of the text effects to create a stencil-like appearance for your text. Here's how to do that:

1. Open the image you want to create the stencil effect in and click the Horizontal Type tool.

2. Add your text to the image.

3. Click the Effects tab and the gallery of effects opens.

4. Click the down arrow next to the box at the upper left of the gallery. Select Text Effects from the list that appears, as you can see in the following illustration:

5. Click the Sprayed Stencil thumbnail and drag it over your text.

6. Elements applies the effect and opens a dialog box to ask if you want to keep the effect.

7. Click Yes to keep the effect.

You can see what the Sprayed Stencil text effect looks like after it's applied to a piece of text by looking at my sample image (see Figure 10-3). It really does look as though you used a paper stencil and some spray paint and got a little sloppy during the painting!

FIGURE 10-3   Here is my image with the Sprayed Stencil text effect applied to the text I added to the image

Fill Text with a Pattern

Here's one more procedure involving a text effect. You can use this procedure to fill text with a pattern. You can't change the pattern, but it's a colorful one, so it would coordinate with a variety of colors. This text effect can be hard to see up against highly detailed images, so for the example image and practice procedure, I'm going to start by creating an empty image window with a white background.

1. Create a new image in Elements with a white background.

2. Type **CONFETTI** in the image area. Use any typeface you want, but use a large typeface so that you can see the effect more clearly. Use at least 36

points. In the following sample image, I used 144-point type so that you could see the confetti pattern details:

3. Open the Text Effects gallery (see the preceding procedure for instructions on how to do this).

4. Click the Confetti (type) thumbnail and drag it over the text.

5. Elements applies the effect and opens a dialog window to ask if you want to keep the effect.

6. Click Yes to keep the effect, which can be seen in the illustration that follows (you can see the pattern—in grayscale—that the Confetti effect creates):

Summary

I bet you didn't know you could do so much with text in Elements or that you could use text to change the look of an image. Now you do! And the fun isn't over yet. In the next chapter, I will show you how to take the skills you learned in this chapter and move them up a level or two. You will also learn how to use text to enhance images and create new looks for those images.

Chapter 11

Create Dynamic Text Objects

How to...

- Add a drop shadow to text

- Make a neon sign

- Outline text

- Emboss text

- Make mirrored text

Now that we've looked into images and text, in this chapter I'll go on to show you how to create some terrific objects using text. I'll also show you how to incorporate these text objects into photographs to come up with distinctive images.

Add a Drop Shadow to Text

You see drop shadows on objects all the time, but rarely do you see them on text. That's because adding a decent-looking drop shadow to a letter or word is hard to do in most illustration programs and impossible to do in page layout or word processing programs. Fortunately, it's a snap to do in Elements, and you get several different drop shadow types, not just one.

I'm going to use one that is really easy to see for this project so that it will show up in the illustrations. Make sure to experiment with the various kinds of drop shadows when you do this project on your own.

1. Open a new file in Elements and make the background transparent by selecting that option in the window that appears when you create a new file. For my illustrations, I used an off-white background to make the drop shadow easier to see in the example images.

2. Click the Text tool and choose a large typeface, at least 36 points.

3. Type **Echo Valley** in the image area.

4. Open the Layer Effects palette (select Show Layer Effects from the Window menu).

5. Click the down arrow next to the box at the upper left-hand corner of the window.

6. Select Drop Shadows from the list and the Drop Shadows thumbnails appear, as you can see in the following illustration:

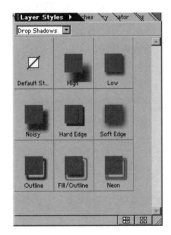

7. Click the High thumbnail. Elements applies the drop shadow, which you can see here:

11

Make a Neon Sign

I love neon signs and think they look great in all kinds of designs. Creating a text effect that looks even remotely like a real neon sign is quite a feat if you're using illustration programs. In Elements, though, it only takes a few steps to make your neon dreams come true. The illustrations in this project are in black and white, but look in the color insert for an example of neon in action.

1. Open a new file in Elements and make the background transparent.

2. Click the Text tool and choose a font that has straight lines and little, if any, curve to the letters. Arial is a good choice if it is installed on your computer.

3. Click the color box on the Options bar and change the font color to a shade of green.

4. Type **Joe's Bar** in the middle of the image area (see the following illustration).

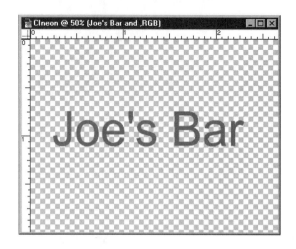

5. Open the Layer Effects palette (Window | Show Layer Effects) and choose Drop Shadows from the list in the upper-left portion of the window.

6. Click the Low thumbnail and drag it over the text. Elements applies a slight drop shadow effect, as you can see in the following illustration:

7. Click the Filters tab to open the Filters palette. Make sure all the filters are showing. If All is not showing in the upper left-hand box, click the down arrow next to the box and select All from the list that appears.

8. Scroll down until you see the Neon Glow filter. Click the thumbnail and drag it over the text object.

9. Elements asks if you want to simplify the layer. Click OK.

10. Elements opens the Neon Glow window, which you can see in the following illustration. Leave the settings as they are and click OK.

11. Open the Layer Effects palette and apply the Simple Emboss and Simple Outer bevels to the object in the order shown. Your image should now look something like this:

11

Create a Text Rainbow

Rainbows make for evocative images. They are colorful, easily recognizable, and sure to bring a smile to someone's face. Here's how to create a rainbow of text that you can use anywhere you want to make someone happy or get someone's attention:

1. Open a new file in Elements and make the background transparent.

2. Click the Text tool and select a typeface that you like.

3. Use a large font size, at least 36 points, and choose a bright color for your type.

4. Type **Over the Hill** just as you see it here:

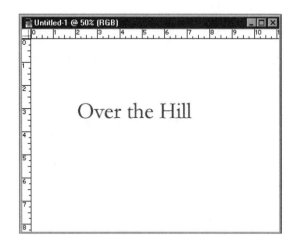

5. Click the Create Warped Text button and select Arch as the style.

6. Click OK and Elements bends the text into an arch shape.

7. Repeat Steps 4–6 twice using a different color for the text each time. If your text curves end up touching each other, as mine do in the image you see here, that's okay. We'll fix that.

8. Move the curves so that they look as though they are standing on top of each other, but don't let them touch.

9. Click the bottom curve to select it and stretch the curve so that it is wider than the other two. Stretch the middle curve of text so that it is slightly wider than the top one.

10. Now push the curved lines so that they slightly overlap, as shown in the following illustration:

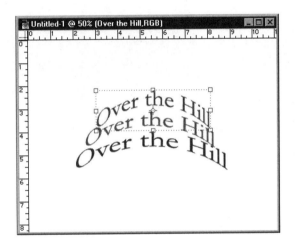

Make Text Translucent

Translucent text is a nice touch to add to an image that has some details in it, but it can get lost when an image has a lot of details. If you want to add translucent text to an image with lots of detail, look for a section of the image that is less busy and add the text there. Here's how to add translucent text to an image:

1. Open the image in Elements that you want to add the text object to.

2. Click the Text tool and add your text to the image. Make the text the size, font, and color that you want to use.

3. Select Show Layers from the Window menu. Elements opens the Layers palette, as you can see here:

4. Click the down arrow next to the Opacity box and adjust the slider so that the text layer is about 50% opaque. If you like the text more solid, make the percentage of opacity higher.

5. Click the Layer Styles tab and click the down arrow next to the box in the upper left-hand corner of the window.

6. Select Outer Glows from the list and Elements shows a collection of thumbnails, as you can see from the following illustration:

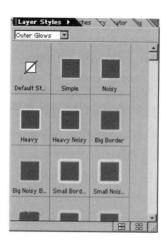

7. Click Big Border and Elements applies an outline to the text object.

8. Open the Layers palette again and change the opacity of the text layer, which has returned to 100%, somewhere lower.

As you can see from the final image (see Figure 11-1), the outline around the text helps draw attention to it in this highly detailed picture. The text and the outline are translucent, thanks to our having lowered the opacity of the text level.

FIGURE 11-1   Reducing the opacity of the text level makes the text and outline translucent

Outline Text Edges

You can see how making text translucent, which you would think would make text less noticeable, actually made the text attract more attention. That's because you did something unexpected. Let me show you how to do something else unexpected with text: apply an outline to the text to make it stand out more.

1. Create a new file in Elements and give it a white background so that you can see the effect more clearly.

2. Click the Text tool and type **Click Here** or any other phrase you'd like to try.

3. Click the Effects tab in the Palette well and click the down arrow next to the box in the upper left-hand corner of the Effects window.

4. Select Text Effects from the list and Elements shows you examples of the text effects, as you can see in the following illustration:

5. Click the Bold Outline thumbnail and drag it over the text. Elements applies the effect to the text.

6. Click the Layer Styles tab to open this palette and apply the Simple Sharp Outer bevel to the text object.

As you can see from the finished example (see Figure 11-2), applying the bevel made the outline effect even more obvious. You don't have to apply a bevel, but it does heighten the effect. You could use any bevel you like, so experiment with various ones.

FIGURE 11-2   Try different bevels—some give a more pronounced effect than others

Emboss Type in an Image

Here's another effect that uses a combination of effects and layer styles, but this one is so different from the others that I want to make sure you know how to do it. You can use this embossing technique to give a raised-letter effect to any object. I am going to use the same sunflower-and-candlestick image I used earlier in the chapter.

1. Open the image you want to add the embossed text to in Elements.

2. Click the Text tool and add the text object to the image.

3. Click the Effects tab and select Text Effects from the list of effects.

4. Click the Clear Emboss thumbnail and drag it over the text object. Elements applies the effect, as you can see here:

11

5. Click the Layer Styles tab and apply the Simple Emboss bevel. Elements applies the effect that you see in the next illustration:

If you like how the text looks after you apply the Clear Emboss effect, stop there. You don't have to apply the Simple Emboss bevel.

Mirror Text

We added a drop shadow to text earlier, which makes a text object look as though it had a shadow. In this project, we are going to create a text object that looks as though it were seeing itself in a mirror.

1. Create a new file in Elements and make the background white.

2. Click the Text tool and switch to the Vertical Type tool. Add some vertical text to the image area.

3. Select Duplicate Layer from the Layer menu. Elements opens the Duplicate Layer box. Click OK.

4. Click the text object and move it to the side, away from the object beneath, as I have done in the following illustration:

5. Select Rotate from the Image menu. Select Flip Horizontal from the list of rotating options that appears. Elements flips the selected text object horizontally.

6. Apply a Medium Outline effect to both text objects. They should now look like the following illustration:

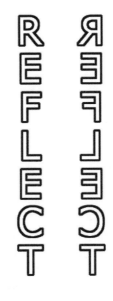

7. Click the Pencil tool, hold down the SHIFT key, and draw a line down the middle of the text objects. That's your mirror!

As you can see in the finished image (see Figure 11-3), the two pieces of text are looking at each other. I used vertical text so that I could draw the line down the middle. I applied an outline effect to the text, but you could also apply any of the procedures for dressing up text that I showed you earlier in the chapter, such as clear embossing or the other text effects.

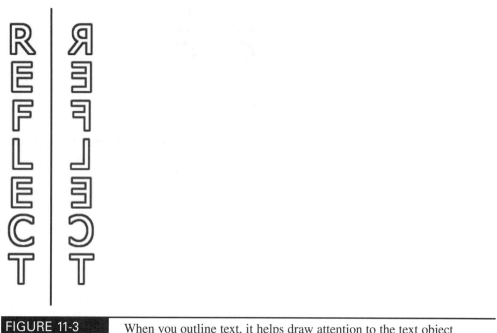

FIGURE 11-3   When you outline text, it helps draw attention to the text object

Summary

We've talked a lot about text objects in Elements, and I have shown you many different ways to take text and make it a graphic. I've also shown you how to add text to an image and given you a few projects that show you what you can accomplish using the text tools. Now, we're going to move on and use a different set of tools. In the next chapter, we're going to talk about the drawing tools in Elements and how you can use them to create images and to change the look of photographs.

Part V

Create New Images

Chapter 12

Enhance Your Images with Drawings

How to...

- Draw a shape
- Create objects using shapes
- Add drawn objects to photographs
- Fill a shape with a gradient
- Use part of a photograph in a drawn object

Elements has drawing tools, the Pencil tool for drawing lines, and a number of tools for drawing shapes. What does the ability to draw lines and shapes have to do with image editing? Can you use shapes to create entire images? Can you use shapes to enhance photographs?

Create a Stacked Object

I am using a simple star shape in this project to show you how you can quickly create unique objects using one shape and a few layer styles. You could use any of the other shapes that Elements will let you create and follow the same procedure outlined as follows.

Once you're finished with your shape, you can use it as a button on a Web site or use it to enhance another image. Or, you could use this procedure to create a Christmas tree ornament! To do that, create the stacked star, print two copies in color, and cut them out. Paste them back-to-back with a loop of string glued between the two stars and you're ready to decorate the tree.

1. Create a new file in Elements and make the background transparent.

2. Right-click the Rectangle tool and the list of drawing tools appears. If you see another drawing tool instead of the Rectangle tool, right-click that tool. The same list will appear.

3. Select the Custom Shape tool from the list. Notice how the Options bar changes when you do this.

4. Click the down arrow next to the Shape box and click the star. The star is one of the custom shapes you can choose to draw with in Elements (see the next illustration).

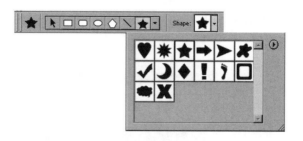

5.   Click the foreground color and select a shade of red to fill your first star.

6.   Click in the middle of the image area, hold the mouse button down, and drag to the right and down. Elements begins to draw the star shape as you do this. Release the mouse button when you have drawn a large star that takes up at least half of the image area. I have almost filled up the image area in the example (see the following illustration).

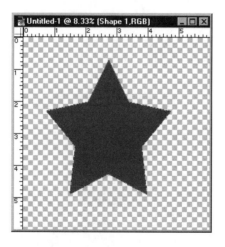

7.   Create a new layer (Layer | New) and call it Green Star.

8.   Click the Foreground Color box on the Options bar and select a shade of green for your next star.

9.   Click somewhere in the image area other than where the star is and draw a slightly smaller star than the red one.

10.   Click the foreground color and select a shade of blue for your next star.

11.   Create a new layer and call it Blue Star.

12

12. Draw another star, this one smaller than the first two. As I have shown next, you do not have to draw the stars on top of each other.

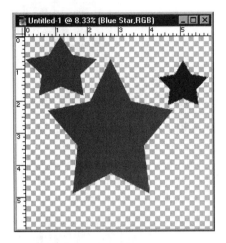

13. Move the stars so that they are layered on top of each other, the smallest on top and the largest on the bottom, as I have done in the following illustration:

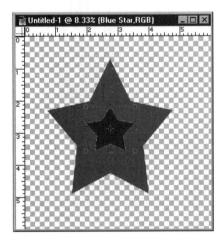

14. Open the Layer Styles palette and select Bevels from the drop-down list on the upper left-hand side of the palette.

15. Click the Scalloped Edge thumbnail and drag it onto the largest star. Elements applies the bevel to the shape.

16. Click the Simple Shape bevel and drag in onto the middle-sized star. Elements applies the bevel to the shape.

17. Click the Inner Ridge bevel thumbnail and drag it onto the smallest star. Elements applies the bevel to the shape. You're finished and you have a stacked star object, as you can see from the finished example (see Figure 12-1).

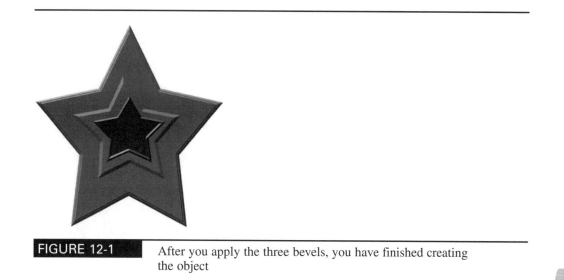

FIGURE 12-1   After you apply the three bevels, you have finished creating the object

12

Create a Checkerboard

In Chapter 8, I had you create a 3-D box using the Rectangle tool, so I won't repeat that exact same procedure here. Instead, I want to show you how you can use the drawing tools in Elements to create easily recognizable objects. In this case, I want to show you how to create a checkerboard, and later in this chapter I will show you a project that uses the checkerboard.

By the way, you can easily adapt this procedure to create any object made up of geometric shapes.

1. Create a new file in Elements with a white background so that you will be able to easily see any background showing through where the shapes meet. For my example image, I used an eight-inch square.

2. If you can't see the rulers on the top and left of the image area, click View and then Show Rulers. You could also use the shortcut on the Options bar to show the rulers.

3. Click the foreground color and select a shade of yellow for your square.

4. Click the Rectangle tool and, using the rulers as your guide, draw a two-inch square in the middle of the image area. You can see that my square is two inches wide by looking at the rulers on the example image (see the following illustration).

5. Select Duplicate Layer from the Layer menu and click OK. You have created a new layer with the same yellow square on it.

6. Repeat Step 5 three times.

7. Open the Layers palette (View | Show Layers). You should have five identical layers and a background layer, as shown in the next illustration. You

will only see one square on the screen, but there are five stacked on top of each other.

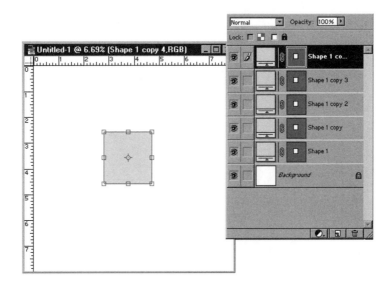

8. Click the yellow square and move it so that it intersects with the upper left-hand corner of the square beneath, as I have done here:

12

9. Click the next square you see and move it so that it intersects with the square in the middle at the bottom left hand-corner of the middle square.

10. See where I am going with this? Good! Take the next two squares and move them so that they each touch the remaining square at one of the corners. You should now see all five squares (see the following illustration).

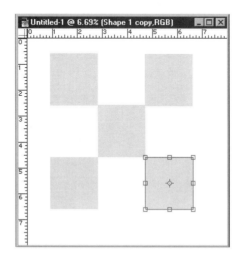

11. Click the Crop tool and select the outer edges of the checkerboard area. Elements shows the crop area but doesn't crop the image.

12. Select Crop from the Image menu. Elements crops the image, leaving only the checkerboard visible, as you can see Figure 12-2.

Did you know?

You can shift the intersection point of the rulers from the upper-left side of the image to anywhere in the image area. If you are drawing in the image area and want to get the dimensions exactly correct, moving the origins around can be helpful. Try it and see. To move the intersection point (0,0), click in the small box at the upper-left side of the screen where the two rulers overlap, hold down the mouse button, and drag the origin point into the image area. Let go when you reach the point where you want the new ruler origin coordinates. To restore them to the default setting, double-click in the small box in the upper-left side of the screen where the two rulers overlap.

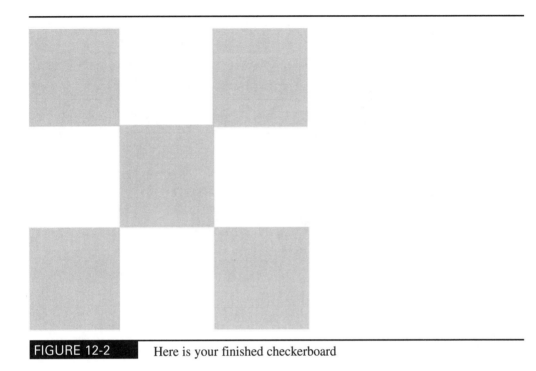

FIGURE 12-2   Here is your finished checkerboard

Footprints in the Sky

I wanted a simple project that would show you how to combine shapes and a
photograph that would also be easy for you to reproduce. All you need to get started is
an image of the sky, so grab your digital camera and head outside to get your shot.
You can also take your regular camera out, take a picture of the sky, and then scan the
resulting photograph. Once you've done that, you can do this project.

1. Open your sky image in Elements.

2. Click the icon for the drawing tool—it doesn't matter which one is currently
    selected. Notice how the Options bar changes when you do this. Look at the
    next illustration to see the Options bar.

3. Click the Custom Shape tool button on the Options bar.

12

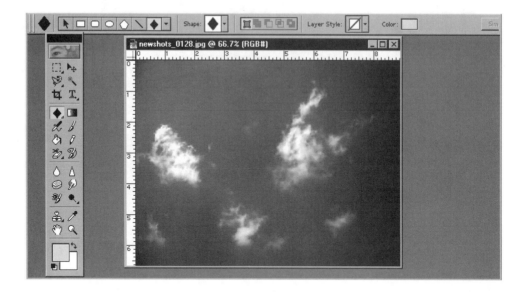

4. Click the down arrow next to the Shape box and the set of special drawing shapes appears.

5. Click the Foot shape.

6. Click anywhere in the photograph and draw a foot. Notice how Elements fills the shape with the foreground color. Notice, too, that you've drawn a right foot, as you can see here:

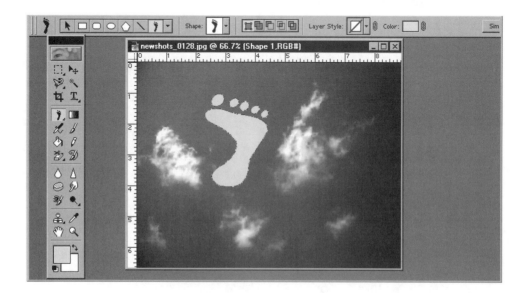

7. Click near and slightly down from the first foot and draw another foot about the same size as the first one.

8. Select Rotate from the Image menu and select Flip Horizontal from the list that appears, as shown next. Elements flips the foot so that it's now a left foot.

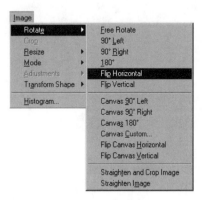

9. Open the Effects palette by clicking the Effects tab. Make sure you are seeing all of the effects by selecting All from the drop-down list located in the box at the upper left-hand side of the palette.

10. Find the Marbled Glass thumbnail by scrolling through the thumbnails. Click the thumbnail to select it, as shown in the following illustration:

11. Drag the thumbnail onto the image. Elements applies the effect, and you get a great-looking and very unusual image, as you can see in Figure 12-3.

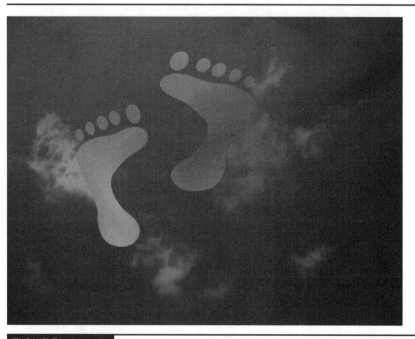

FIGURE 12-3   The footprints show up well after you've added the marble effect

Create a Custom Bullet Point

People use bullet points all the time in presentations. Graphic designers also use them as decorative items for headlines, dividers, and symbols such as the dot at the end of a magazine article. Once you start looking for bullet points, you'll see them everywhere. You can use the bullet points that come with the presentation or page layout software you're using, but you can also create your own using the drawing tools in Elements.

The particular bullet point I am going to show you how to create has a pattern fill, but you could fill the shape with a solid color. The fill is totally up to you!

1. Create a new image in Elements with a transparent background.

2. Click the drawing tool that is currently active. Click the Ellipse tool button on the Options bar.

3. Click the down arrow next to the Custom Shape button. The Ellipse Options dialog box appears.

4. Click Circle to make Elements draw a circle instead of an oval. You can see the selection in the following illustration:

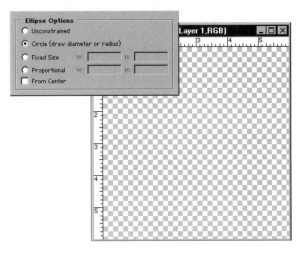

5. Click in the image area and drag to create a circle. Elements fills the circle with the foreground color, but we'll change that later.

6. Click the Move tool and click the circle. Resize the circle if needed, so that it occupies most of the image area.

7. Select Fill from the Edit menu and the Fill window appears.

8. Click the down arrow next to Custom and the palette of fill patterns opens, as you can see here:

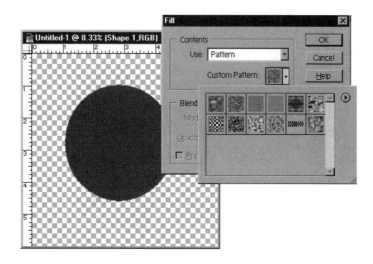

9. Click the Wood thumbnail. Elements applies the fill to the circle.

10. Open the Layer Styles palette and apply the Simple Emboss bevel to your circle to smooth the edges of the circle. You can see the Bevel choices here:

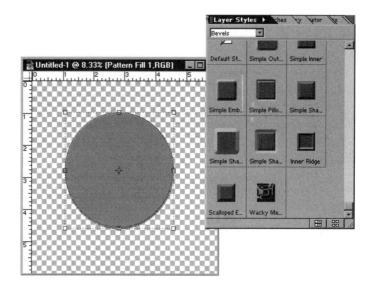

Use the Checkerboard

I am going to show you two examples of how to use the checkerboard that you created earlier in the chapter, but I also want to point out that you can use the checkerboard to create a border around an image. All you have to do is copy and paste the checkerboard sections until you get a complete border.

In this first project, I am going to show you how to use the checkerboard to create a tic-tac-toe game using the drawing shapes in Elements. In the second project, I will show you how to use sections of another image to create game pieces for the checkerboard.

Once you see these finished images, I am sure you will be able to come up with ideas of your own on how to use these kinds of images. However, let me get you started brainstorming by suggesting using a tic-tac-toe game as a graphic for a presentation or in an advertisement. It would be effective anytime you want to illustrate a winning strategy or indicate the game is over.

1. Open the checkerboard image in Elements.

2. Choose black as your foreground color.

3. Click a drawing tool and click the Custom Shape button on the Options bar. The gallery of custom shapes opens.

4. Click the X shape and Elements changes the Options bar, as shown next:

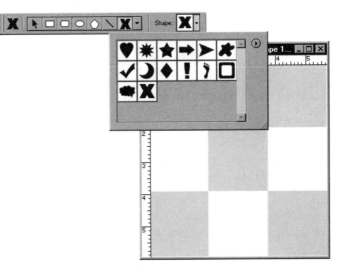

12

5. Click in one of the white areas of the board and draw an *X*. If you didn't get the *X* in the middle of the square, click the Move tool and move the *X* to the center of the white square.

6. Repeat Step 4. You now have two X marks on the board.

7. Click the Text tool and add a circle to one of the yellow squares by typing an uppercase *O*. If the letter isn't round enough for you, try another typeface. I used Lucida Console for my *O* (see the following illustration).

8. Add more *X*s and *O*s until you get the game to the level you want.

Use the Checkerboard, Take 2

In this project, I'll show you how to create game pieces using a photographic image. As I suggested earlier, the checkerboard is a versatile image. You can use it to create game-related images, or you can use it as a border or background.

1. Open the checkerboard image in Elements.

2. Open the photograph you want to use to create the game pieces in Elements. Arrange the windows so that you can see both images side-by-side, as you can see next:

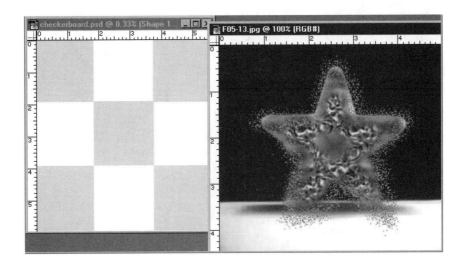

3. Right-click the Rectangular Marquee tool and switch to the Elliptical Marquee tool.

4. Select a small circular portion of your photograph using the Elliptical Marquee tool. Try to find an interesting portion of the image. I used part of the star.

5. Select Copy from the Edit menu.

6. Click the other image and select Paste from the Edit menu. Elements places the copied area into your checkerboard.

7. Resize the dot if necessary. I resized mine after I pasted it in so that it's in proportion with the squares, as you can see here:

12

To finish off your game board, you can copy another circle from the photograph or create a solid color circle using one of the colors from the first piece. Then, apply a different bevel to each game piece and you're all set. Figure 12-4 is my example image of a checkerboard with a game in progress.

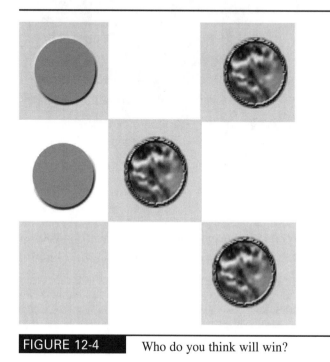

FIGURE 12-4   Who do you think will win?

Summary

Elements lets you change the look of your photographs, but it also contains a whole collection of shapes and drawing tools that lets you creatively change your images—and create new ones out of shapes alone. What a bonus to have in an image-editing program! I hope you explore further how to use the shapes in Elements to create, edit, and change images. To help you do that, I've provided another chapter on shapes that shows you even more of the shapes that come with the program and how you can use them. That's next!

Chapter 13

Put Simple Shapes to Work

How to...

- Add a communicative touch to an image
- Make directional arrows
- Create an award
- Frame a picture
- Hide shapes in a picture

Now that you've learned how to draw a shape, fill it, and incorporate it into an image, it's time to learn how to use your drawing skills to enhance all sorts of images. I want to show you the multitude of special shapes you can use to spice up your images.

Add a Communicative Touch to an Image

Sometimes you take a picture that is perfect for adding a thought or a word balloon to. Any action picture, especially one with a child or a favorite family pet, is a good choice for this procedure, outlined as follows:

1. Open the image in Elements.
2. Right-click the Rectangle tool and choose the Custom Shape tool. Or you can just hold the Rectangle Tool icon down to get the shape options to appear.
3. Click the down arrow next to the custom shape box.
4. Click the small arrow button on the window that appears and a list of custom shapes pops up, as shown next:
5. Select Talk Bubbles from the list and Elements changes the examples to show the talk bubbles.

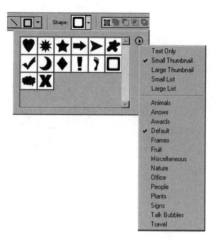

6. Click the Thought2 bubble and click anywhere in the image.

7. Draw a thought bubble large enough for a short message.

8. Fill the bubble with a light color (or white). Rotate the bubble and size it, if needed.

9. Click the Text tool and add your text.

10. Change the opacity of the layer the thought bubble is on so that you can see the text and some of the detail behind the bubble. As you can see from the finished example image (see Figure 13-1), you can personalize images easily this way.

FIGURE 13-1   Paw-Paw is how you say Granddaddy in the Deep South…just so you know

13

Whip Up a Butterfly

Throughout this book, I have shown you how to create fun images, and one of the images I used early in the book for us to have fun with was that of a butterfly. I used a photograph of a butterfly sponge, but here I want to show you how to use a shape to create your own butterfly.

1. Create a new file in Elements and make the background transparent.

2. Click the Rectangle tool and select the Custom Shape tool.

3. Open the list of custom shapes and select Animals from the list.

4. Click the Butterfly2 shape and click in your image area.

5. Draw a butterfly shape like the one you see here:

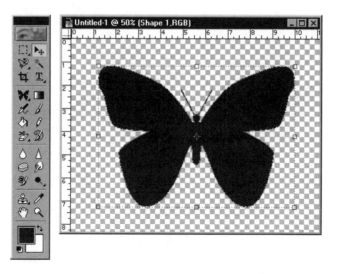

6. Fill the shape with the Satin fill (Edit | Fill | select the Satin fill).

7. Right-click the Custom Shape tool and select the Ellipse drawing tool.

8. Draw some circles on the butterfly's wings as I have done in the next example. Click the Paintbrush tool and add some stripes to the wings.

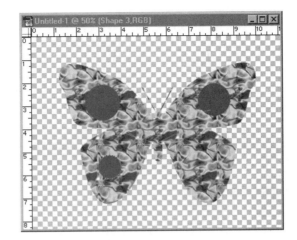

You can see from my finished butterfly (see Figure 13-2) that you can be as fanciful as you like when you create your butterfly. You could also copy the markings of a real butterfly to get a more realistic-looking creation.

FIGURE 13-2   I added some dots and lines to the wings of my butterfly

13

Create a "You Are Here" Symbol

You have seen a "You Are Here" symbol on maps, especially maps in the local shopping mall. You can use the following procedure to create one for any map that you'd like to make, or you can print it, cut it out, and paste it on a real map. You can also have a lot of fun with the procedure once you've learned it. You could create any symbol you want using the same technique. In fact, later on in the chapter, I'll show you how to create another useful symbolic image using the same idea.

1. Create a new file in Elements, make it a small square, and make the background transparent.

2. Right-click whatever drawing tool is active and select the Custom Shape tool.

3. Open the list of custom shapes and select Signs from the list of shapes.

4. Click the Sign 8 thumbnail as I have done here:

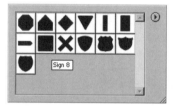

5. Click in the image area and draw a rectangle. Notice that the edges are rounded.

6. Open the list of custom shapes and click Sign 9.

7. Draw an X in your box that is a little smaller than the box.

8. Fill the X with a contrasting color.

9. Click the Text tool and add the text "You Are Here" to the image. As you can see in the following image, I'm not finished typing yet:

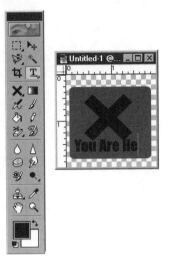

Point the Way with a Directional Arrow

Elements gives you more than a few arrows, some simple and straightforward and others a little more curvy and complex. Any one of the arrow shapes will do for this procedure. If you want to use the directional arrow along with the You Are Here symbol, use one of the colors in the You Are Here symbol in the arrow to help coordinate the two.

1. Open a new file in Elements and use a transparent background.

2. Open the list of custom shapes and select Arrows from the list. Elements displays a set of thumbnails of different arrow shapes.

3. Click the thumbnail for Arrow 9.

13

4. Draw the arrow in your image, as shown in the following illustration:

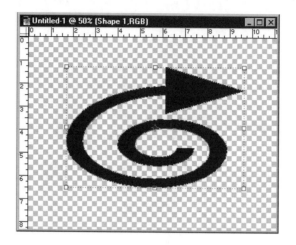

5. Fill the arrow with the pattern of your choice.

6. Click the Text tool and add "This Way" to your arrow point.

7. Select a Warped Text shape for your text (click the Warped Text button and select a shape); as you can see here, I chose the Fish shape:

8. Bevel your shape (Layer Styles Gallery | Bevels) and add a text effect (Effects Gallery | Text Effects) to the text, if you want, to finish the arrow.

I used the Inner Ridge bevel on my arrow and the Brushed Metal special effect on the words on my arrow. Look at the finished arrow in Figure 13-3 to see the end result.

FIGURE 13-3   I used a bevel and a special effect to complete my arrow

 Need a set of arrows that look alike but point in different directions? Make one arrow, copy it as many times as needed, and rotate it in whatever direction or angle you need it to point by using the Image | Rotate controls. Once the arrows point where you want them to go, you can make small changes to the arrows to customize them slightly, if desired.

Make an Embossed Award

13

I have filled the middle of this award with part of an image. You could do the same, or you could fill the center of the award with a color, a pattern, a fill, or anything else you can think of. Once you are finished with your award, you can paste it into another image or print it, cut it out, and pin it on someone's shirt! This is a great project for awards of any kind, birthdays, or any celebration that you want to make extra special.

1. Open a new file in Elements that is larger than the size of the award you want to create. Make the background transparent.

2. Open the list of custom shapes and select Awards.

3. Click the Ribbon thumbnail and draw a ribbon shape in your image area.

4. Fill the shape with the color or fill of your choice. Blue is a nice color for ribbons, so try blue if you don't have another preference.

5. Open the image that you want to copy a portion of and copy that portion. Use an elliptical marquee for your selection area. Close the photograph.

6. Paste the copied section of the image onto your ribbon, as you can see in the following image:

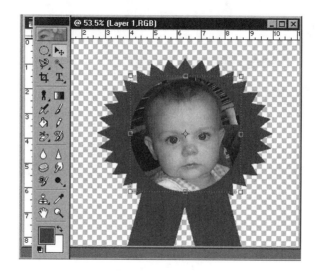

7. Add vertical text to the ribbons of the award. You will have to rotate the text slightly to get it to fit properly. Try white for the color of the text. It will show up nicely against the blue of the ribbons.

8. Emboss the ribbon with your choice of bevels.

I added one of the Layer Effects called Outer Glow (Fire) to my embossed ribbon, as you can see in the finished image (see Figure 13-4). Now I am ready to print the ribbon and hand it to the little girl's granddaddy so that he can wear it with pride!

FIGURE 13-4   In case you were wondering, I'm the great aunt!

Frame a Picture

I have shown you several ways to frame a picture by using shapes or the special effect
frames in Elements. They were simple box frames and they look great. But there is
more than one way to frame a picture in Elements! Let me show you another way
using one of the custom shape frames. You could use any of the custom shapes; I'm
going to use one of the more detailed ones in this procedure:

   1.   Open the picture you want to frame in Elements.

13

2. Open the list of custom shapes and select Frames from the list.

3. Click Frame 14 to select it and click in the image area.

4. Draw your frame in the image area.

5. Resize your frame so that it fits around the edges of the image.

6. Pick a color from the image to fill the frame with or use the fill of your choice.

7. Experiment with the various drop shadows (Layer Effects | Drop Shadows). Apply them to the frame until you get a look you like.

I applied a drop shadow and a few other layer effects to get the image to look as it does. As you can see from the finished image (see Figure 13-5), the frame doesn't cover up all the edges.

If you want your frame to cover the image, copy the section of the image that would fit within the frame and paste that section into a new image. Copy the frame and paste it on top of the copied section; adjust both as needed. Discard the edits and frame in the first image.

FIGURE 13-5   I like this look, where the frame doesn't cover the entire image—but you can fix it to do so

Make a Warning Sign

Stop, *no*, and *don't* are all emphatic figures of speech, but they take on greater urgency when we turn them into images. Using the shapes in Elements, you can create your own No symbol from any image. I am going to create a simple symbol, but you could easily combine the No symbol with a photographic image. For example, you could take a picture of someone smoking and put that symbol over the cigarette.

1. Create a new file in Elements.

2. Open the list of custom shapes and select People from the list.

3. Click the Walk1 shape and draw that shape in your image.

13

4. Color the shape black, as you can see in the following illustration:

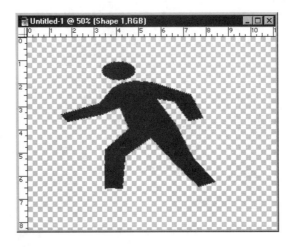

5. Select Miscellaneous from the list of custom shapes.

6. Click the No Symbol thumbnail and draw the shape in your image area.

7. Fill the shape with a high-intensity shade of red and resize it as necessary until it completely covers the shape beneath.

As you can see from my completed image (see Figure 13-6), I have enlarged the No symbol until you can see enough of the shape beneath to get the general idea. I have also added bevels to both shapes to give their edges some additional definition.

Create an Eye-Catching Paper Clip

This is a fun project that you can use with other images once you have finished creating your attention-getting paper clip. I like the idea of using the finished object in an advertisement somehow or anywhere where you want someone to pay attention to what you are showing.

1. Create a new file with a transparent background in Elements.

2. Open the list of custom shapes and select Office from the list.

3. Click the Paper Clip thumbnail and draw one in the image area.

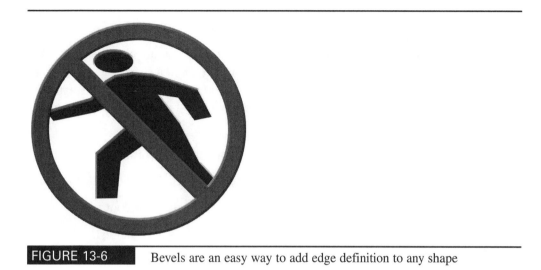

| FIGURE 13-6 | Bevels are an easy way to add edge definition to any shape |

4. Rotate the paper clip. Apply the Outer Glow/Radioactive Layer effect to the paper clip.

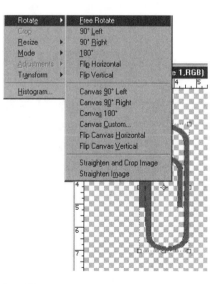

5. Apply a bevel to the clip.

When you use the paper clip in an image, you will need to erase the part of the paper clip that would be under the paper or image. Slide a paper clip onto a sheet of paper at the same angle as your paper clip image so that you can see what part of the image to cut away.

Design Your Own Stamps

I used the paper clip shape from the Office set of custom shapes to create the image in the last procedure. In this procedure, I am going to show you how to use another office shape to create your own stamp. I am using a simple shape and a letter on my stamp, but you could use anything you could copy and paste—including your company logo or a letter.

1. Open a new file in Elements with a transparent background.

2. Open the list of custom shapes and select Office from the list.

3. Click the Stamp thumbnail and draw a stamp shape in your image area.

4. Open the list of custom shapes and select Plants from the list.

5. Click the Flower 2 thumbnail, as shown here:

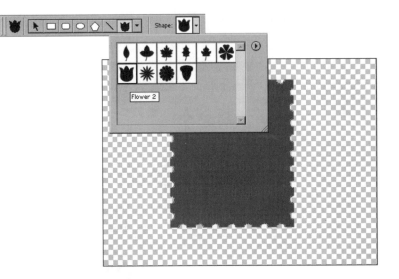

6. Draw a tulip in your stamp and color it some color other than the stamp color.

7. Click the Horizontal type tool and select one of the Symbol or Wingding typefaces.

8. Find some letters that look like abstract shapes and use them to decorate your tulip. Use a color that contrasts sharply with your tulip.

9. Add a text effect to the letters and a different one to the abstract shape letters.

10. Add a bevel to the tulip and the outer edge of the stamp.

11. Use the Add Noise filter on the whole image and you're done!

My finished image (see Figure 13-7) is a fanciful version of a regular stamp, but you can create any kind of stamp you want. I suggest you start your own stamp collection using stamps you've created in Elements.

FIGURE 13-7   You could create your own stamp series to commemorate important family or office events

TIP   *Create your own gallery of shapes and shape combinations by creating a lot of small files using one shape in each image. Then, use the Contact Sheet II capability (File | Automate | Contact Sheet II) to create a printed gallery of the shapes. That way, you won't have to look them up all the time; you'll have the shapes at your fingertips and can share them with others more easily.*

13

Carve Out a Logo

In this project, I want to show you how to combine a drawn shape, two custom shapes, and some letters to create a logo. I created similar images for the color insert section of this book, where you can see what the color images from a procedure like this would look like.

1. Create a new file in Elements with a transparent background.

2. Draw an oval in the middle of the image area. Fill it with the fill of your choice, but try something metallic-looking like Molecular fill (if you don't like another fill better).

3. Open the list of custom shapes and select Frame 15.

4. Draw a frame around the oval so that none of the oval shows.

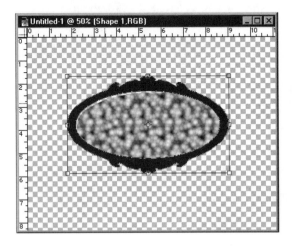

5. Select Nature from the list of custom shapes and click the Sun 4 thumbnail.

6. Click inside the oval area of the image and draw a sun. Move the sun shape so that it is in the upper part of the oval.

7. Color the sun a bright yellow.

8. Use the Horizontal Type tool and type **KBK** under the sun.

9. Center the letters under the half-circle portion of the sun.

10. Adjust the opacity of the fill layer downward so that the sun and the letters are the most prominent part of the logo.

As you can see from my finished logo (see Figure 13-8), adjusting the opacity of the fill layer is a really good way to make the text and the sun image stand out more. You never want the background fill to overpower the rest of the image.

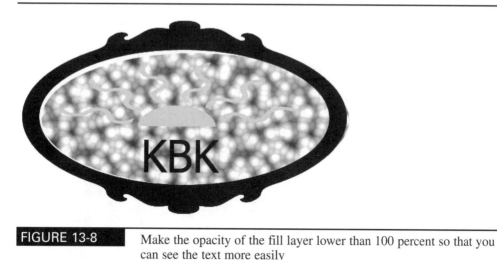

FIGURE 13-8	Make the opacity of the fill layer lower than 100 percent so that you can see the text more easily

Hide Shapes in an Image

This is a good project to do if you want to make a game for younger children to play. You hide small shapes in a photographic image and ask them to find the shapes and circle them. You could use the same idea to come up with an activity for adults to do during a training session. Use different shapes, of course, but follow the same procedure. Don't use a photograph with a lot of detail to it, in any case. If you do, the shapes can get lost in the details and the game/activity will be too difficult or time-consuming to do.

1. Open the photograph in Elements.

2. Zoom in so that you fill most of the screen area with the image.

3. Select one of the categories of custom shapes. I used Animals for my example, but you could use any category. Stick to one category or two related categories, though.

13

4. Click the thumbnail of one of the shapes and draw the shape somewhere in the image.

5. Click another thumbnail and draw another shape in the image.

6. Repeat Step 5 until you have all the shapes in the image you want to have.

As you can see from the finished image (see Figure 13-9), it's a good idea to rotate shapes and hide them under things so that they are harder to find.

FIGURE 13-9   Add shapes on the walls, on people's heads, everywhere you can think of

Summary

We've reached the end of the section of the book where I show you how to edit and create images. Now, we're going to move on to learn how to do some of the necessary housekeeping duties that come along with working with images. For example, you need to learn how to prepare your images for the Web and for print. You also need to learn how to export your images so that you can give them to people in the format they need for their work.

It's been a lot of fun up to this point, but don't worry—the fun isn't over yet. I am going to show you how to get the most out of your images, now that you know how to change and make terrific images. How else could you get the most out of Elements?

Part VI

Share Your Images with the World

Chapter 14

Save and Export Images

How to...

■ Choose a file format for saving images

■ Export a file

■ Check an image's dimensions

■ Reduce file size and resolution

■ Save important information about an image

Learning how to save your files is as simple as clicking the floppy disk icon on the toolbar, isn't it? Yes and no. Click the icon and you will save your file, but do you know in what file format? Do you know what file format it should be in?

In this chapter, I want to answer questions such as these. I will tell you about which file formats are appropriate for various situations and how to choose among the various options for saving and exporting files. What I have to tell you is not something you can pick up by following menu and keyboard shortcut commands, but it is vitally important in learning how to use Elements.

Once I outline some the basic information you need to know about saving and exporting files in Elements, I will walk you through procedures related to the topic under discussion. I will take you step-by-step through the procedures, pointing out significant information and settings along the way. Please take the time to look through the material in this chapter; you may be familiar with the general process but not all the details.

My discussion about file formats is generic—in other words, you can use it for any computer program you're using. The other material in this chapter is specific to Elements, so it may or may not apply to other software programs. Many programs work along similar lines, so you may be able to transfer some of the knowledge you learn in this chapter to other programs. Just don't be surprised if you can't!

Save vs. Save As

There are two different ways to save files inside of Elements. Both are available from the File menu, as you can see in Figure 14-1. (There is also a Save For Web option, but I talk about that option later in the book.)

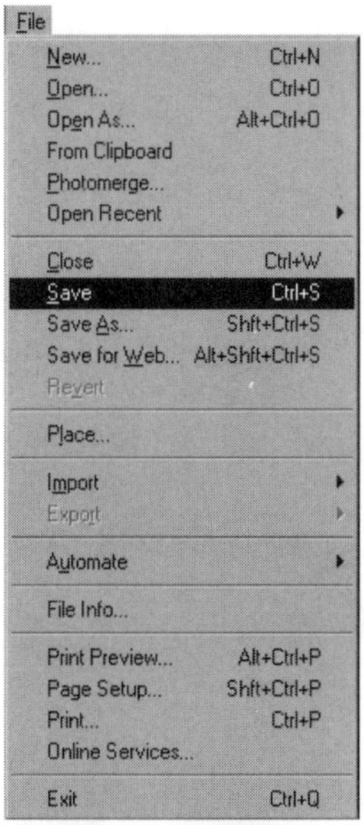

```
File
  New...              Ctrl+N
  Open...             Ctrl+O
  Open As...          Alt+Ctrl+O
  From Clipboard
  Photomerge...
  Open Recent                    ▶

  Close               Ctrl+W
  Save                Ctrl+S
  Save As...          Shft+Ctrl+S
  Save for Web...     Alt+Shft+Ctrl+S
  Revert

  Place...

  Import                         ▶
  Export                         ▶

  Automate                       ▶

  File Info...

  Print Preview...    Alt+Ctrl+P
  Page Setup...       Shft+Ctrl+P
  Print...            Ctrl+P
  Online Services...

  Exit                Ctrl+Q
```

FIGURE 14-1   Both Save and Save As are on the File menu

When you save a file in Elements and you choose the Photoshop file format, you are telling Elements to take all the components of the file, including all the objects and all the layers, and tuck everything away into a digital storage box. When you want to edit the file again, you open the Photoshop file, where you can access all the bits and pieces of your image. If you use another file format when you save images (except for those listed as follows), Elements will change or discard parts of the image (such as the layers). Thus, you may not be able to edit all the parts of an image unless you save it in the Photoshop file format—with the exceptions listed as follows.

I admit that having two options for saving files—Save and Save As—can be confusing. Why include two ways to do one basic function? Both work the same way, but having both available can help you keep your file organization scheme straight, as I will explain in the two sections that follow.

Save a File for the First Time

When you save a file for the first time, you need to stop and think about where you want to store the file. If you've done your prep work, you've probably created a folder or two for the project. If not, before you save a file, you might want to stop and create some new folders first. Then, you can follow the following procedure to save the file.

1. With the file open that you want to save, choose Save from the File menu.

2. The Save As dialog box opens—the same dialog box is used for Save and Save As.

3. Check the file destination in the box at the top of the window. Change the destination if necessary.

4. Type a filename in the File Name box. Leave the file format as Photoshop.

5. Click Save. Elements closes the box and saves the file.

6. Notice that the filename at the top of the image window has changed to the filename you typed in the File Name box.

Some important details to notice here: After you save a file for the first time, Save on the File menu is grayed out, as is the floppy disk icon on the options bar. They will stay that way until you make a change to the file. Then you can save the file again using the Save command or clicking the floppy disc icon. Save As is always available.

When you save the file again, Elements will save the file to the file destination you used when you saved the file the last time. So, remember to set up folders for your projects before you get started, and always save the files inside those folders.

Using Save lets you set up your saving destination for a file, but what do you do if you want to save the file to another location or destination at some point? Say you have finished working on a file and want to save one on the local network server so other people can use it. You also want to keep a copy of the file on your computer's hard disk, which is where you have been saving the file all along.

When you want to save the file to another place or with another name or file type, you use Save As. It's simple: Use Save to save the file initially and set up the file destination and name. Use Save afterward while you are working. Use Save As after you have saved the file at least once using Save when you want to make changes to the name, file type or file location.

The box that appears when you choose Save As looks just like the box that appears when you choose Save. It is the same dialog box! Don't hit the Save button, though, until you have made the name, destination, or file format changes that you want to make.

How to ...   Manage Your Save Routine

To keep things straight in my own mind, here's my procedure for saving files when I am using Elements. I am passing the information along to you in the hopes you will create your own similar saving routine:

1. Before I start a project, I set up folders for the images for that project on my hard disk.

2. I save the file in Photoshop format while I am still working on it. Saving periodically while you are working is a good idea in case you want to go back to an earlier version of the image. It's also a good way to prevent losing your work if you need to reboot the computer while you're in Elements.

3. When I am finished working on the file for a while or I have completely finished my work, I save the file in the Photoshop format. If I need to save the file in another format because someone needs the file in that particular format, I use Save As to create that file.

File Format Options

As you can see in Figure 14-2, Elements lets you save files in a number of file formats. I've already told you about some of the benefits of saving your files in Elements' native file format, Photoshop. I have also told you how to save a file in that, or another, format. Now, I want to tell you about some of the other file formats available in Elements and why you might want to choose one or another.

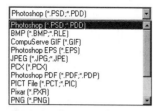

FIGURE 14-2   There are lots of different file formats available to you in Elements

When you save an Elements file in a file format other than Photoshop, you are exporting the file—even though there is no Export option in the program. I am telling you this because sometimes when people ask you for a file, they will ask you to "export" it in a particular file format. If they ask you to do that, they are asking you to "save" the file "as" that format.

You will see as I walk you through saving files in various formats that Elements sometimes gives you file options when saving. I will point these out to you and tell you how to make decisions about the important options.

Making Decisions

The different file formats have various advantages and disadvantages. For example, saving a file as a Tagged Image File Format (TIFF or TIF) image gives you a file that word processing and other image editing programs can open and edit. However, TIFF files tend to be large, especially when the image is in color.

You need to make some decisions before you decide on a file format (or formats) to use when saving a file. Before you save a file in a format other than Photoshop, take a few minutes before you save and do a mental check. Doing this will help you pick the most appropriate file formats for your image. Ask yourself about all the ways you will want to use the file once you've saved it—will it be included in a document that will be printed on a printing press, will you use it for the Web, or do you want to make the file size small enough to fit on a floppy?

You can always go back later and save the Photoshop file in another format, if you need to have the file in another format that you hadn't thought to use earlier. I think it's a more organized way to work, though, to save the file in several formats that you know you will need later once you have finished editing or creating the file.

File Format Guide

In Table 14-1, I have listed many of the most common file formats, all of which are supported by Elements. As I just outlined, it's a good idea to get into a routine of saving your files in the same formats—say, Photoshop and some other format. You can always open the Photoshop file and save it in another format later if you need to, but saving it in Photoshop and another file format as you work gives you plenty of flexibility.

Name and Abbreviation	Use When	Windows Extension
Encapsulated PostScript (EPS), shown on list as Photoshop EPS	You need an image with a preview; the image will be printed on a printing press; you need to open the image in an illustration program	.eps
Graphic Interchange Format (GIF)	If the image is a simple one without lots of colors (not a photograph) and you want to use it on a Web site	.gif
Joint Photographic Experts Group (JPEG)	If the image is a photograph or has lots of colors and you need to use the image on a Web site, show it on a computer screen, or e-mail it to someone	.jpg, .jpe
Portable Document Format (PDF), shown on list as Photoshop PDF	You need a file someone can read with Acrobat Reader or open in Acrobat or other Adobe application	.pdf, .pdp
Tagged Image File Format (TIFF)	The image you started with was a scanned image or a digital camera image, or you want a file format that just about any program can open	.tif, .tiff

TABLE 14-1   Common File Formats That You Can Use in Elements

While TIFF is one of the most versatile image file formats, there are a few others that Elements supports that most other programs can open, including BMP, PCX, and PICT. The other file formats you see listed on the available file formats are used by graphic arts professionals under a limited range of circumstances.

File Size Comparison

I have explained what the different file formats can be used for—use this information when deciding what file format is appropriate. I want to tell you now about how the file format selection can affect the size of the file. The best way for me to do that is to show you two files that I created in Elements and the resulting file sizes when I saved them in various formats, including Photoshop.

A file's resolution has a lot to do with its final, saved file size. If you start with a high-resolution scanned or digital image (anything 300 dpi or higher), the file size is going to be large when you save the file. You're dealing with a lot of image data with these kinds of images! If you create a simple object using the shapes in Elements and use a file with a low resolution (such as 72 dpi), the saved file won't be that big.

Check a File's Size (Dimensions and Resolution)

Before I show you the file size comparisons, let me tell you how to check the resolution of the image. Remember, the larger the resolution, the larger the file will be. Later in the chapter, I will tell you about ways you can reduce a file's size before and after you save it.

1. Open the image in Elements and select Resize from the Image menu.

2. Select Image Size from the list that appears. The Image Size box appears.

3. Look at the number in the Resolution box.

4. Click OK to close the window.

Figure 14-3 shows an image that I took with an inexpensive digital camera. The original image is about 3 inches wide and 2.5 inches tall and is 96 dpi.

The Photoshop file is 175KB. I saved the file in the various file formats shown in the table, and here are the file sizes I got:

EPS	GIF	JPEG	PDF	TIFF
325KB	40KB	18KB	62KB	231KB

FIGURE 14-3   This picture, taken with a digital camera, is only 175KB

Quite a difference in file sizes—as you can see. One of the reasons the file sizes are so different is that some file formats, such as EPS, save information about the image or a thumbnail preview of the image along with the image data. Some file formats, such as GIF and JPEG, reduce the amount of data saved for the image according to parameters you set when you save the image.

Here's another example, using a 4″ × 6″ photograph that I scanned at a much higher resolution (see Figure 14-4). I used part of this image in the color insert section of this book and so scanned the whole picture at 450 dpi.

FIGURE 14-4   I scanned this image at 450 dpi and got a file size that is many megabytes in size

I started out with a TIFF image, just as I did with the digital camera image. When I saved the original TIFF image as a Photoshop file, I got a file that was about 12,000KB in size. Just a few more numbers: the EPS file was almost 10,000KB because I included a preview file, but the JPEG was 1,155KB. As I said, different file formats use different ways to save the data and thus result in different file sizes.

> TIP
> *When you set up your file folders and start saving files, think up a set of commonsense names that you can use when you save your files. Relate the folder names and filenames to the name of the project—or the date— or something else that is connected with the project and makes sense to you. Having a bunch of files named Photo1, Photo2, etc., makes it a lot harder to remember which files go with which projects.*

Reduce the Resolution of an Image

When you create a file that will be used in print (that is, will be printed on a printing press), the higher the resolution the better—topping out around 600 dpi for most images. Always check with the company that is doing the printing or the graphic artist you are working with to see what resolution they want the images to be. You must scan the photograph using 300 dpi or higher resolution or use a digital camera with a high enough resolution, because as good as Elements is, it can't create image data out of thin air.

You can use the procedure I am about to show you to increase the resolution of an image, but don't bother trying to increase it more than about 10 percent. The resulting image won't look very good when it's printed—remember, you need the image data (resolution) going in.

However, you can (and should) reduce the resolution of an image if you want to make the file size smaller—say, to fit a file on a floppy disk, or if you are going to e-mail a file to someone or post it on a Web page. I will talk more about what to do with images destined for the Web in Chapter 16, but for now let me just tell you that a resolution between 70 and 100 dpi works fine for Web and e-mail images. That's because computer monitors only display that many dots per inch on the screen.

Reduce Image Resolution

When you reduce image resolution, you make the file size smaller by reducing the number of dots that Elements can use for the image. Reducing image resolution is a good thing to do if your images will be shown only on the Web or if you are trying to send someone a sample image via e-mail and you need to make the file size smaller.

1. Open the image in Elements and select Resize from the Image menu.

2. Select Image Size from the list that appears. The Resize box opens.

3. Type the desired image resolution in the Resolution box.

4. Click OK. Elements closes the box and changes the image resolution.

Never change the resolution of an image and save the new file with the same name as the original. Give the new file a different name—maybe the original name plus the resolution (Acme72, for example). If you do this, you will never groan in frustration when you realize you really did need to keep that higher-resolution file to use again.

> TIP
>
> *You don't have to change the resolution of a file to make it smaller if you use a file compression utility after you save the file. Programs that compress files can reduce file sizes without making a big difference in how the files look. These programs are free (freeware) or cost only a small fee to use (shareware). Check them out if you don't already have a favorite file compression utility.*

Save a File in TIFF Format

Now that we've talked about file formats and sizes, I want to show you two procedures. Each saves a file, and each touches on different options for saving. This first procedure walks you through creating a TIFF file.

1. Open the file in Elements and choose Save As from the File menu. The Save As box opens.

2. Choose TIFF from the list of file formats.

3. Type your new filename in the File Name box. If you leave the name the same on the PC, it's okay; you'll just get two files with the same name and different extensions. On the Macintosh, though, you may copy over the original file.

4. Click Save and the TIFF Options box opens. You can see the box in the following illustration:

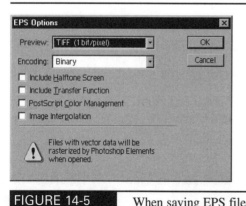

5. Select IBM PC if the image will be used only on a PC. Otherwise, select Macintosh.

6. Click OK and Elements saves the file and closes the box.

Save a File in EPS Format with a Preview

When you save a file in EPS format, you select PostScript EPS from the list of file types. Elements will then present you with the EPS Options box, which you can see in Figure 14-5. I want to show you the box because there are some scary-looking options listed. Unless you have been instructed by the graphic artist or printing company to include some of these options in the file, do not bother to select any of them. When in doubt, take a screen shot of the box and send it to them for their expert opinion as to what you should do.

FIGURE 14-5   When saving EPS files in Elements, leave the options unselected unless someone has told you to select one or more

Change Saving Preferences

I bet you didn't know that you can change some of your settings for saving files as preferences. Yes, you can, and doing so will help save you time when you are working with a large number of files and saving them. Here's how to change your saving preferences:

1. With or without a file open, choose Preferences from the Edit menu in Elements.

2. Select Saving Files from the list that appears. The Preferences window appears.

3. Make changes to the settings as desired. For example, as the following illustration shows, you don't need to always save a preview with every image.

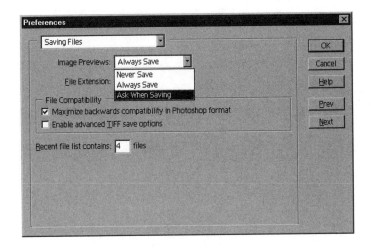

4. Click OK to save your changes and close the box.

How to ...   Save Valuable Information about an Image

This feature lets you save information in much the same way as you would if you turned over a photograph and wrote on the back! You can print the information you add to an image, too. I will show you how to do that in the next chapter. To save information about an image, select File Info from the File menu and type your caption in the box in the File Info window. Click the down arrow next to the box at the top of the window to find other categories of information you can add (see Figure 14-6). When you're finished, click OK to save the information and close the window.

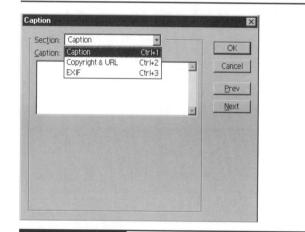

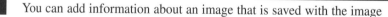

FIGURE 14-6   You can add information about an image that is saved with the image

Summary

Now that you've learned that there is a lot more to saving files in Elements than you thought, it's time to move on to another topic: printing your files. Saving and exporting files lets you leave your images in digital format and hand them on to others. Printing them is another way to share your images with the world, and I've got a lot to tell you about this topic, too.

Chapter 15

Print Your Images

How to...

- Scale an image to fit the paper

- Print part of an image

- Print multiple copies of an image on the same page

- Print one layer of a multilayer image

- Print the caption for an image

- Make your print match what you see on screen

Printing images is one of those tasks, like saving images, that is easy to do; you select Print from the File menu and away you go, right? It is that easy, but if you want to get consistently good print results and take advantage of the features embedded in Elements related to printing, you'll want to read this chapter.

First, I want to give you short explanations and definitions for some of the printing-related terms you'll encounter in Elements. You'll understand your options better after you know what these terms mean. Then, I will tell you about why what you see on screen isn't always what you see on paper after you print an image and how to get the best printed image from Elements.

In the last part of the chapter, I want to tell you about the cool print features and options you have with Elements. You can, and should, use these features as you work with the program—doing so will make your life easier and your printed images better! I'll walk you step-by-step through these procedures, pointing out important options along the way.

Printing Terms

There are a few terms that you will see in the Print Preview, Page Setup, or the Elements help files that may cause some confusion. So, let me explain what these terms mean:

- **Bounding Box** Elements puts this border around an image print preview to show you where the image area ends.

- **Color Management** Elements manages the print parameters of an image so that what you see on screen and what prints are as close to an identical match as possible.

- **Crop Marks** Elements puts these small marks around the edges of the image area to show you where the image area stops. If you want to trim the paper around the image area away, printing an image with crop marks is a good way to get a guide for those scissors!

- **Dot Gain** When a drop of ink touches a piece of paper, it spreads a little. That's dot gain. How much the drop of ink spreads has a lot to do with how porous the paper is and how thick the ink is, but no matter what, ink drops always spread to some degree. When they spread too much, they can run into other areas of color on the page and create hybrid colors that you, and the printer, don't want to see. Controlling dot gain is something the printer—the person, not the computer hardware—needs to worry about. You will see the term "dot gain" in the Help files for Elements, but all you need to know is what it is. Don't worry about trying to control it. Let your printer do the worrying for the both of you.

- **Gamut** When something "runs the gamut," it starts at the beginning and goes to the end. The term "gamut" is used in color printing to indicate the full spectrum of colors that can be printed. Your monitor can show you colors that can't be replicated on a printing press or an inkjet or color printer. Taking steps to get the closest match between your monitor's gamut and the output device's gamut is part of the art and science of color management.

> **TIP**
>
> *You can make any image look better by using the right kind of paper when you print the image. If you are printing color photographs and you want them to look like photographs, use glossy photo stock paper. If you are printing any color image on an inkjet printer, use good quality inkjet paper. It's worth investing in high-quality laser printer paper, too, whether you have a color or black-and-white laser printer. The bottom line: never use photocopy paper on anything other than your photocopier!*

15

Print an Image with Crop Marks

As I mentioned earlier, crop marks show you where you can cut (crop) the excess paper away from the image area. For example, your image might be two inches square, but your image area could be four inches square. If you measured from the

crop mark to the edge of the image, you'd have one inch all the way around. Here's
how to print an image with crop marks:

1. Open the image in Elements.

2. Choose Page Setup from the File menu. The Page Setup box appears.

3. Look at the bottom of the box. Click the box that says Corner Crop Marks to
    turn this option on. In the illustration, notice I have clicked the box already.

4. Click OK. Elements closes the box. When you print the image, the crop marks
    appear on the paper.

Print Part of an Image

This is a cool feature in Elements that will come in handy when you have a large
image and you want to print it in pieces. Or, if you want to show only a section of an
image to someone, you can print out just that section.

1. Open the image in Elements that you want to print part of.

2. Use the Rectangular Marquee to select the area of the image you want to print.

3. Choose Print Preview from the File menu. The Page Setup box opens.

4. Click the box next to Print the Selected Area. You can see I have done that in the next illustration. The preview will not change to show only the selected area.

5. Click Print and the Print box opens.

6. Click OK to print the selected area.

How to ... Print One Layer of a Multilayer Image

Normally when you print a multilayer image, Elements prints one image showing all the layers, stacked on top of each other. If you want to print only one of those layers, open the Layers palette (Windows | Show Layers) and click off the views of the layers you do not want to print. Then select Print from the File menu; only the visible layer will print.

15

Print a Background on an Image

You can automatically put a background on an image that shows up only when the image is printed. Using this print feature is a good idea if you want to create different images and frame them with a background only when they are printed. This is a particularly good thing to do if you are printing more than one image per sheet of paper and want to make it easy for people to see where one image stops and another begins.

Let me warn you, though, that if you put a background on a single image and print one image per page, Elements fills the rest of the page outside the image area with the background. That can be a lot of color if you're printing a small image.

1. Open the image in Elements and select Page Setup from the File menu. The Page Setup box opens.

2. Click Background and the Color Picker box opens.

3. Select a color for the background by clicking a color in the window. Elements closes the Color Picker window.

4. Click OK on the Page Setup box; the box closes.

5. Choose Print from the File menu. The Print box opens.

6. Click OK to print the image with the background in the color you've chosen.

Put a Border Around an Image

Adding a border to an image that shows up only when the image prints is another way to finish off an image when printing it. The border is a box that prints around the image, and you can control the width of the border when you add it to the image. Adding a border makes the image larger—much larger if you create a wide border—so keep that in mind if you want specific overall image dimensions. You would use a border for the same reasons you use a background when printing an image.

1. Open the image in Elements and choose Page Setup from the File menu.

2. Click Border. The Border box opens.

3. Enter the width of the border in pixels. Any number higher than 5 makes a really thick border. You can see the Border box in this illustration:

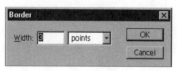

4. Click OK. Elements closes the window.

5. Click OK on the Page Setup window.

6. Select Print from the File menu and print your image with its border.

Scale an Image for Printing

When you print an image, you sometimes want to enlarge it or shrink it to fit on a single page. This is particularly true if you have created an image larger than a letter-size sheet of paper and want to fit the image on one piece of paper so that you can show it to someone else. Here's how you can automatically scale the image to fit the paper. Note, too, that most printers are not able to print every square inch of the paper—they need some room at the top or bottom of the page to move the paper through the printer.

1. Open the image in Elements.

2. Choose Print Preview from the File menu. The Print Preview window opens.

3. Click the box next to Scale To Fit Media, as I have done in the next illustration. Notice how Elements has enlarged the image to fit the letter-size page.

4. Click Print to print the scaled image.

15

How to ...

Control the Amount the Image Is Scaled When It's Printed

Normally an image prints at 100% of its size, but you can change that. Open the Print Preview box (File | Print Preview), change the 100% figure to whatever percentage you'd like, and click Print. Instant enlargement or reduction at your fingertips!

Change the Position of the Image on the Page

Elements automatically centers the image on the page horizontally and vertically, but you can position the image to print anywhere on the page that you want it to print. This is a handy feature to use, say, if you are printing greeting cards on card stock and want to control precisely where the image prints on the upper or lower portion of the card.

1. Open the image in Elements and open the Print Preview box.

2. Notice that there is a check mark in the box next to Center Image.

3. Click that box to remove that setting.

4. Type in the new position data in the Top and Left boxes. Use a negative number to move the image to the bottom or left. Look at the following illustration for an example of what happens when you use negative settings:

5. Click Print to print the image where you have designated.

Print the Caption for an Image

In the preceding chapter, I showed you how to attach information to an image, such as a descriptive phrase (a caption) or copyright information. This information appears when you select File Info from the File menu. You can also print it when you print the image. Here's how to do that:

1. Open the image in Elements.

2. Choose Page Setup from the File menu. The Page Setup box appears.

3. Click the box next to Caption.

4. Click OK to close the window.

5. Choose Print from the File menu and print the image. The caption appears centered beneath the image.

 *You don't always have to select Print from the File menu. You can also click on the Print icon on the option bar to get the whole printing process started.*

Print Multiple Images per Page, Option 1

Earlier in the book, I told you how to print more than one image per page. I wanted to tell you again, step-by-step, how to do that in this chapter, so that you will have all the print-related information in one spot.

1. Place all the images you want to print on contact sheets in the same file folder.

2. Start Elements (you don't need to open a file).

3. Choose Automate from the File menu.

4. Choose Contact Sheet II from the list that appears. The Contact Sheet II window opens.

5. In the Columns box, type in the number of images you want to go across the page.

6. In the Rows box, type in the number of images you want to go down the page.

15

7. Click Choose and the Browse For Folder box opens.

8. Locate the file folder you placed the images in.

9. Click OK when you have selected that folder; the box closes.

10. Click OK on the Contact Sheet II button and Elements prints the images as instructed.

As you can see in Figure 15-1, I have set up the Contact Sheet II box to print 12 images per page. You can tell that from the numbers I typed in, but you can also tell that from the preview shown at the right-hand side of the box.

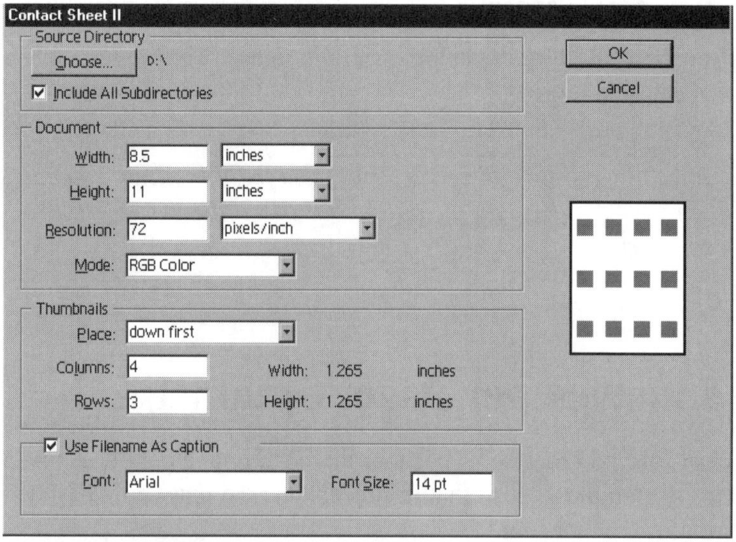

FIGURE 15-1   I told Elements to print four columns and three rows of images

Print Multiple Images per Page, Option 2

There is another way to print more than one image per page, but you have to put the images into the same folder the way you did in Step 1. This method lets you control the final printed size of each image more precisely. You are limited to the various layout options listed, but there are a lot of them. You're sure to find one you can use.

1. Put the images you want to print as a set into the same file folder.

2. Select Automate from the File menu.

3. Select Picture Package from the list that appears. The Picture Package box opens.

4. Click the down arrow next to the Layout box and choose the image layout that you want to use. As you can see from the illustration, there are lots of choices.

5. Click the layout you want to use. Elements shows you a preview of the image layout when you click one of the layouts.

6. You can also choose to alter the print resolution and print in grayscale by changing the settings on the box.

7. Click Choose and tell Elements where the file folder is that contains the images you want to print as a group.

15

8. Click OK when you have made your selections and desired changes. Elements creates a new file with the images laid out as you have instructed.

You can print the same image multiple times on a single sheet of paper if you click the Use Foremost Document box underneath the Choose button. Then you end up with something like Figure 15-2. You set up the number of images on the page when you choose the image layout.

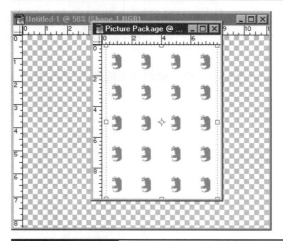

FIGURE 15-2   Elements will print a sheet of paper with multiple copies of the same image

How to ...   Print a Color Image in Black and White

If you have an inkjet printer or color laser printer and want to print a color image in black and white to save your color ink or toner supplies, you can easily print the image in black and white. You don't have to convert the image to grayscale first. Just look in your printer manual for instructions on how to tell the printer to print in grayscale rather than color and follow those directions.

Change the Color Management Profile

As I explained earlier, sometimes your computer monitor can display colors that an output device can't replicate. If, when using Elements, you find that the image you see on screen is not what comes out of your printer, first check your monitor's calibration as I explained in the first part of this book. If you have never done it, do it now. If it's been weeks or months since you calibrated your monitor, do it again. The settings slip after a while, so you need to do it routinely.

If calibrating your monitor doesn't bring the screen and the output colors closer together, you can try changing the color management profile for your printer. Here's how to do that:

1. Open the image in Elements and choose Print Preview from the File menu. The Print Preview window opens.

2. If the Show More Options box isn't checked and you don't see the Background and Border options, click the Show More Options box.

3. Click the down arrow next to Output and choose Color Management from the list that appears. The Print Preview box changes to what you see here:

15

4. Click the down arrow next to the Profile box and a long list of profiles appears. Choose Printer Color Management from the list.

5. Click Print, print your image, and see if the problem has disappeared or lessened.

6. If you're still having a problem, repeat Steps 3–5 and choose a monitor profile. If you see the name of your monitor on the list, choose that profile. If not, choose a profile that is the same manufacturer as your monitor. When in doubt, try the Wide Gamut RGB profile.

Summary

As promised, I've told you a lot about the different printing features and options available to you in Elements. There's a lot more to printing than just clicking the printer icon, isn't there? I urge you to try out these different options when you're printing your images. They aren't hard to do and can sometimes save you valuable time and bothersome frustration. Now, we're going to move on to the other segment of this part of the book—preparing your images for Web use. We've covered printing, so now let's tackle making your images look their very best on Web sites.

How to...

- ■ Optimize your image for the Web or e-mail
- ■ Choose the best file format for your image (Web or e-mail)
- ■ Choose the best compression method for Web images
- ■ Animate an image file
- ■ Create a Web photo gallery

Here we are! This is the last chapter, but since you're probably not reading the book straight through the way you would a novel, this may be the first chapter you've turned to. No problem. Whether this is the first chapter you've read or you're working your way systematically through the book, whatever route you took to get here is okay. You're here and that's all that matters.

This chapter is an important part of the segment of the book on sharing your images with the world because so many people want to be able to share their digital images on a Web site or send them as part of an e-mail message. In this chapter I want to tell you how to use the features and capabilities built into Elements that will help you get the best images you can for Web use. That means good-looking images that don't take a long time to download or send electronically.

Another exciting feature in Elements is the ability to put together photo Web pages using your digital images. Once you have created these pages, you can add them to a Web site. I will walk you through the entire multistep process, one set at a time.

Before we get into the how-to portion of this chapter, I want to fill you in on what happens to your images when displayed in a Web browser. Then I will define a few terms for you and give you the information you need to make informed choices that affect file size and image quality. When we're finished with all the background information you need to know, I'll get straight down to business and tell you, step-by-step, how to use the functions in Elements to prepare your digital images quickly and reliably for the Web, or to send them to someone via e-mail. In fact, everything I tell you in this chapter about images will serve you well whenever you need to prepare images that will be seen only on a computer monitor.

Images on the Web

You want your images to look their best whether they are seen on paper or on a monitor screen. When images are displayed on a monitor, there are considerations and limitations that you need to know about so that you can work around them as much as possible. I will briefly list the information you need to know about images on the Web here:

- Web browsers and e-mail programs interpret the colors that are in your image—they do not merely relay the color information in the file to the screen. They can also reduce the number of colors in an image. Different browsers and e-mail programs handle colors differently—there is no standard way to handle color in images.

- The text that you create in an image in Elements is treated as part of the graphic and not as a separate piece of text. That means that your text may be hard to read if you use small (less than 12-point) type in your image. If it's too large, say 60 points or larger, it may look choppy around the edges. Leave text out of Web-bound images or stick to medium-range point sizes.

- The smaller the file size, the faster the image will load onto your Web page or be transferred via e-mail. Keep in mind that monitors can't display a higher resolution than 100 dpi unless they are special display screens. So you can decrease file size without compromising the visible image quality—I'll demonstrate that later on.

- Images look different on different monitors; an older monitor may not display colors as well as a newer one.

- The way an image looks on a PC monitor can be remarkably different from how it looks on a Macintosh monitor. Since you started off the book by using the Adobe Gamma utility, your images look terrific—but keep in mind the other folks in the world who don't have access to such tools.

Now, I know that after reading this list, you're probably thinking that you have no control over the way images appear on screen. That would be true if you didn't have Elements, or an equally capable software program, to help you solve or reduce these problems. I wanted to tell you about these problems so that you can understand how to put the rest of the information in this chapter to good use.

16

Important Terms

You will see these terms on the various dialog boxes and windows in Elements when you are working with images destined for the Web. You may encounter others as you read through the Help files about Web and e-mail images. These terms are not everyday, common language, so I want to fill you in on what they mean and why you should pay attention to them when you see them in Elements.

- **Browser Dither** What the browser does with a color it has no direct match for—it comes up a color using the colors it can display.

- **Compression** The act of making a file smaller, usually described as lossless (no loss in image quality) or lossy (some loss in image quality).

- **Indexed Color** A color palette in Elements with 256 colors.

- **Optimization** Preparing an image for the Web so that there is an acceptable trade-off between its appearance and its file size.

- **Palette** The set of colors than can be assigned to an image.

- **Pixel Dimensions** The number of pixels that make up the image's horizontal and vertical measurements.

- **Web Colors** The set of colors that most Web browsers support.

One of the ways you can prevent problems with browser dither is to use only colors in Elements that are Web colors—which makes them "Web safe." In Figure 16-1, you can see what the Color Picker looks like after I activated the Only Web Colors feature by clicking the Only Web Colors box. When you do that, Elements will only allow you to pick Web colors.

File Format Options

When the Web started getting popular a few years ago, Web developers decided that new image file formats were needed for Web and screen-destined images. So, a few committees got together and came up with some new standards. I could write a whole book detailing the debate about the best uses of these file types, but instead I'll give you a few words about each. I will also tell you when I think you should use each type—based on my own experience with these file types.

- **GIF** Graphics Interchange Format is a file format that gives you lossless compression but is limited to 256 colors (it is an indexed color format). I use the

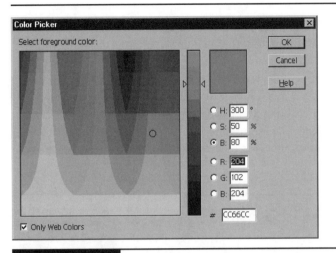

FIGURE 16-1   When you select Only Web Colors, the Color Picker will show you only Web-safe colors

GIF file format only for graphic images such as the logos I created for the color section of the book. It works just fine when you have only a few colors (fewer than 256) in your image and not many shades of colors. I do not use it for photographic images with lots of color range. A transparent GIF is one in which the background is transparent, which allows the Web page background to show through the GIF image. You can also animate GIFs to create an image that moves. I will show you how to do that later on in this chapter.

■ **JPEG** Joint Photographic Experts Group is a lossy compression file format that can greatly reduce the size of a file without making the image look bad on screen. I use this file format for photographic images on the Web exclusively. A progressive JPEG is one that appears progressively as the image data is being downloaded, rather than waiting for the entire file to be received before anything is displayed. Great idea, but some Web browsers don't support this file format.

■ **PNG** Portable Network Graphics is a lossless compression method that has many of the same features as GIF. It's a newer file format than GIF, though, so it is not as widely supported, browser-wise. I have started to use it instead of GIF, but I am careful to check the browser support and don't use it if I know the people visiting the site are apt to have older versions of browsers. PNG-24 gives you more colors in an image than PNG-8, so I always use PNG-24 when I use PNG unless the image has fewer than eight colors and color shades.

16

Just so you know, because other people may mention they do this, you can use file formats such as BMP, TIFF, and PCX for Web images. However, these file formats are intended for print and are not optimized for Web use. I stick to the three image file formats (GIF, JPEG, and PNG) for Web graphics.

I want to show you what can happen to a very colorful photograph when you save it in GIF format. In the image here (see Figure 16-2), which is a photograph I used in Chapter 14, the color range has been abbreviated by saving it in the GIF format. The effects of the reduction in color range are particularly noticeable in the area beneath the bridge. Look closely and notice a lot of detail that you would expect to see isn't there.

FIGURE 16-2   Look closely at the image—the details under the bridge are harder to see now that the image is a GIF file

Achieving Optimal Web Images

As promised, now that we are finished with the necessary introductory material, it's time to get down to actually making some of this Web image preparation happen. I want to start off by showing you a neat feature built into Elements that helps you optimize images by showing you before and after views in the same window.

Then I want to show you how to make dither work for you rather than against you, how to work with GIFs, and then how to check out and reduce cross-platform image display problems. When you get finished with this chapter, you'll know more about optimizing images for the Web than many Web designers learn after months on the job.

JPEG Compression and Quality Trade-offs

As I explained earlier, you want to have the fastest possible download times for a Web image—you don't want to have people staring at a screen full of image placeholders waiting for the images to load. However, you want to preserve as much of the image quality as you can. It's a delicate negotiation you're going to have to set up when you optimize images for the Web. Fortunately, Elements gives you a neat tool for making side-by-side comparisons of file size versus image quality.

I have called this section "JPEG Compression" because of my recommendation that you use only JPEG with photographic images. However, the procedure I am about to outline works the same way for GIF and PNG images.

1. Open the image you want to optimize in Elements.

2. Select Save For Web from the File menu. The Save For Web box opens.

3. If JPEG is not showing in the Optimized File Format box, click the down arrow next to the box and select JPEG from the list of file formats.

4. Elements shows you a portion of the original image on the left and then a preview of the same section of the image as it would look with the image

settings indicated. As you can see from this illustration, the JPEG setting is on 44 (medium quality):

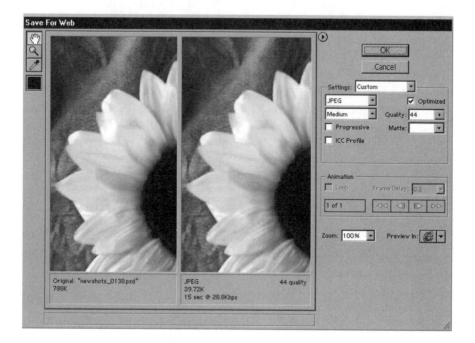

5. Notice the file size and approximate download time shown under the sample on the right. Your job is to get the best-looking image quality balanced with the fastest download time.

6. To do this, try a lower quality setting. Click the down arrow next to the Compression Quality box (the default setting is medium). Select low from the list that appears.

7. If you are not happy with the low setting, click the down arrow next to the Quality box (the one that said 44) and use the slider that appears to adjust the quality level upward. You can see the slider here:

8. As a final check, select Maximum from the Compression Quality list (see Step 6).

9. When you've found your ideal balance of image quality and download time, click OK and Elements closes the Save For Web box.

10. The Save Optimized As window opens. Tell Elements where to save the file and click OK to save the file and close the window.

> **TIP**
>
> *Before you make your final selection, use the Hand tool (upper left-hand corner of the Save For Web window) to move the image around in the preview window. Click in the original section of the previews, hold the mouse down, and move the preview around. The optimized preview will move at the same time. You can also change how much you see of the two images by clicking the down arrow next to the Zoom Level box and selecting one of the views from the list that appears.*

To use Save For Web to preview and save GIF and PNG images, follow the same procedure, except change the Optimized File format to the file type you want to use. See Step 3 for details on how to do this.

16

As you are looking at your images, you may want to jot down the various quality levels and resulting download times. Doing so will help you make decisions about relative trade-offs. What's three seconds faster if the image quality looks a lot worse?

TIP *For making your Web images look better after you've optimized them: 1. Preview the images in various browsers and edit the color content of the images as needed; 2. Use the various sharpen filters to take away some of the fuzziness that conversion to JPEG and GIF can cause; 3. Reduce the number of colors in the image to a workable minimum and make sure those colors are Web-safe; 4. Finally, add a drop shadow or frame around the image to draw attention to it, if needed.*

Check Out Browser Dither

As you work on optimizing an image, you can check to see the effect that browser dither would have on the image. There are ways to reduce the dither if you discover during your dither preview that it has a major detrimental effect on your image.

1. With the Save For Web box open, click the triangle (button with a triangle on it) to the upper right of the two previews. A list appears. You can see the list in the next illustration.

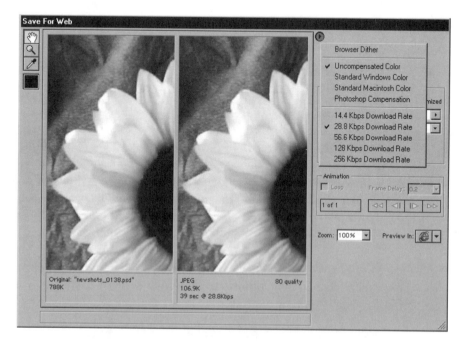

2.   Choose Browser dither and Elements changes the preview to show you the amount of dithering that will occur if you use the file and other image settings you've selected when you save the image for the Web.

Did you know?

Did you notice that when you click the triangle button, a list of modem speeds appears on the list underneath the display choices? If you want to change the modem speed used for the estimated download times, open this list and choose your alternate transmission speed.

Reduce Browser Dither

If you find that the amount of dither in the image is too much for your tastes, you must replace the more dither-prone colors in your image with Web-safe colors. In other words, exit the Save For Web procedure, open the Color Picker, switch to Only Web Colors, and use those colors in your image. As you can imagine, this is a time-consuming process, but it's very effective. Here's another way to reduce browser dither that takes less time but is not as exacting:

1.   Open the image in Elements and choose Mode from the Image menu.

2.   Choose Indexed Color from the list that appears. The Indexed Color box appears.

3.   Click the down arrow next to the Palette box and choose Web from the list that appears, as you can see I have done here:

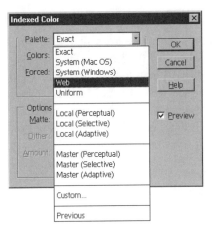

16

4. Click OK to save the image with its Web-safe colors.

There are some options for dithering (none or type of dither), plus the amount of dither and other settings you can experiment with on the Indexed Color box (see Figure 16-3). These settings appear after you've chosen Web from the list. If you are not happy with the look of your image after you have switched to Web colors, experiment with these various settings to see if you get a look you like better.

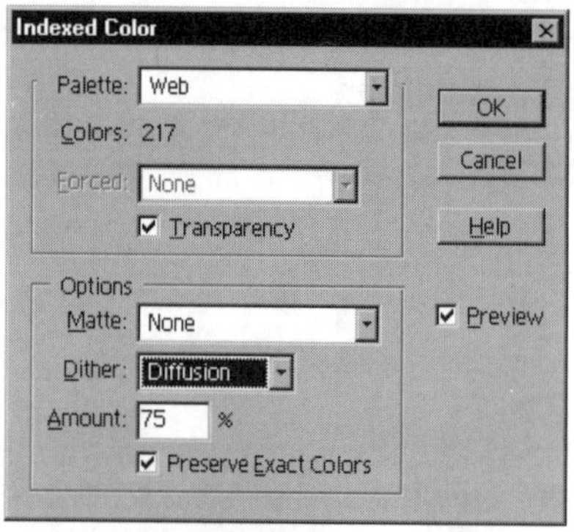

FIGURE 16-3   Experiment with the Indexed Color settings to get the best-looking image you can

> **TIP**   *There are various dither and Web color settings available (only a few, really) on the Save For Web box. Click the down arrow next to the Named Optimization Settings box to see this list.*

Preview an Image in a Browser

After you've saved the image in a Web-ready format and checked out the dither, it's time to do one more check of the image. This step is optional, and you may want to skip it unless image fidelity is a top priority. If it is, you will want to preview your image in a browser to see what it will look like once it's on a Web page.

If you have a browser installed on your computer, Elements lets you launch the browser from inside Elements with a click of a button. You can preview the image as you are working on it or after you have saved it.

1. Open the image and open the Save For Web window (the second part of this step is necessary if you're not currently working on the image).

2. Notice the button next to "Preview In" on the lower right-hand side of the box. The icon for a Web browser should be on the button. If the browser you want to preview the image in is not shown, click the down triangle next to the button and choose the browser you want to use.

3. Click Preview In.

4. The browser software is launched, and the image appears in the window, as you can see here:

5. Close the browser window to return to the Save For Web box in Elements.

If you have more than a few files to convert to a Web-ready file format and you aren't picky about the settings, remember you can use the Batch command to automatically convert a set of images to a particular file format. You can always use the Save For Web process after the conversion to tweak the images.

16

Animate a GIF

When you animate a GIF, you set it up so that when the image appears on the Web page or when someone clicks it, it starts to move. Animated GIFs are very popular, but some image editing programs don't let you add the extra animation touch to GIF images. Elements makes it easy to do that, though. Also, don't let yourself get stuck thinking of animation only in terms of images—you can create animated text GIFs in Elements, too. Just use text instead of images when you create the file. Otherwise, the process is the same.

You must start by placing each frame (action) of your animation on a separate layer. For example, to make a ball bounce, you must make separate layers for the ball at rest, the ball falling, and the ball bouncing up. Once you have created one layer per action for the animation, you can animate the image by following this procedure:

1. Open the image in Elements and select Save For Web from the File menu.

2. Choose GIF from the list of Optimized file formats.

3. Click the Animate box to start the animation process. Elements changes the options on the window, as you can see here:

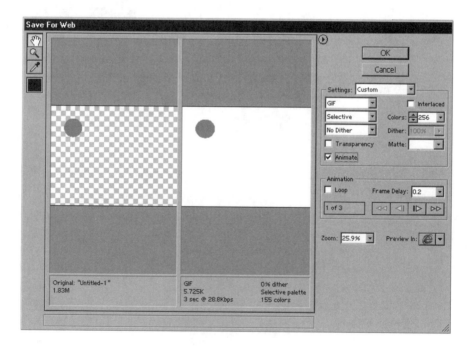

4. Click Loop if you want the animation to repeat itself over and over. If you don't click this box, the animation will play only once after it is activated.

5. You can delay the start of the next layer (frame) by no seconds up to 10 seconds. Type in the amount of delay between layers in the Frame Delay box or click the down arrow next to the box to select your time.

Just so you know, if you use the Save As option on the File menu and choose to save the multilayer file as a GIF, you get the same options for animating and viewing as you do when you open the Save For Web box.

How to ...   Preview a GIF Animation

You can preview a GIF animation while you are working on it. I recommend you do this to get the timing of the slides correct. You are looking for a nice transition—nothing so fast a person could blink and miss something important. And nothing so slow they are annoyed waiting for something to happen. After you have clicked the Animate box and set the timing, use the controls beneath the frame delay box. They work like VCR controls and allow you to view the animation a frame at a time, see the whole animation, stop, and rewind.

Background Work

Have you ever seen an image on a Web page where the background of the image didn't match the color of the Web page? That, as the English would say, is bad form in Web design. You want to set up your images so that there are no background surprises. Most of the time, especially with GIF images, that means making the background transparent when you first create the image in Elements.

But what do you do when you are handed an image or you take one with your digital camera and you need to take care of some background issues? Let me tell you about a few ways to handle backgrounds in Web images.

16

Make the Background Transparent, Option 1

If you're not sure whether the background of an image is transparent, try previewing the image in a browser, as I told you earlier how to do. If you see a background, then you can—sometimes—remove the background so that the edges of the objects blend into the Web page background. Here's how to do that:

1. Open the image in Elements.

2. Click the Background Eraser tool.

3. Click the image and erase the background of the image.

4. Zoom in, if necessary, so that you can get into the tight spots around the object.

Make the Background Transparent, Option 2

If the background of the image is all the same color or similar colors and those colors are different from the colors used in the objects in the image, you can make the background disappear in a different way. You can combine this method with the method I just described and knock out just about any background you come across.

1. Open the image in Elements.

2. Click the Magic Eraser tool and click somewhere in the background of the image. Elements erases the pixels around where you click.

3. Raise the Tolerance setting to have Elements select only pixels that more closely match the color of the ones you just erased.

4. Repeat Steps 2 and 3 until the background is gone (or mostly gone).

When you erase part of an image so that there is no background—and thus that part of the image is transparent—Elements gives you a visual clue that you have accomplished the deletion correctly. As you can see in Figure 16-4, the transparent area shows as a gray-and-white checkerboard. The white area around the dot is what remains of the background. I could have used the Magic Eraser and gotten rid of the all the background in seconds because the background is one shade of white—but I wanted to show you some background pixels!

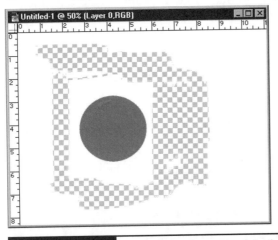

FIGURE 16-4   I erased only a part of the background—the transparent areas are indicated by the checkerboard

 When you have finished removing the background from an image, make sure to save the image as a GIF or PNG and click the Transparency box to preserve the transparency of the background.

Make a Blend-in Background

If you find that it is too difficult to erase the background of an image because the object's edges are too finely detailed or objects overlap, you can create a background that is the same color around the edges as your Web page. This way, you can take your irregularly shaped object, create a box around it, and blend the rest of the background into the Web page. This is not a hard procedure to carry out once you have done it a few times, but I would not recommend it over erasing the background. To do this method correctly, you need to know the exact color of the Web page background as expressed in one of the color schemes you see on the Color Picker window.

1.   Open the image in Elements and use one of the Custom Shapes to draw a boundary around the object(s). Doing so will give you an eraser guide and help you preserve the portion of the background around the object.

16

2. Use the Eraser tools (Magic and Background) to erase (carefully) the area outside the shape you have drawn.

3. Delete the shape.

4. Select Save For Web from the File menu. The Save For Web box opens.

5. Select GIF or PNG as the file type.

6. Click the down arrow next to the Matte box and choose Other from the list that appears. The Color Picker window opens.

7. Type in the RGB formula or one of the other color scheme formulas for the color you want.

8. Click Preview In to see the results of your work.

9. Save the newly matted image as a GIF or PNG file.

How to ...   Check Image Colors (PC/MAC)

I mentioned earlier that PCs and Macs can display an image radically differently. You can check for such differences on a particular image, and you should, if you know that people looking at the page or e-mail photo will be using one or the other kind of computer. To look at the previews, open the Save For Web box with the image open in Elements. Then, click Preview Menu (upper right-hand side of the box) and select the preview (Standard Windows Color or Standard Macintosh Color) that you would like to check. If, when you check the two appearances, you see differences you don't like, you can change colors in the image to indexed colors and check the previews again.

Create a Photo Web Page

As promised, I want to show you a really fun and easy method for automatically arranging your images on a page so that you can post that page on a Web site. This is a simple way to take all those digital images you've worked so hard on through this book and make Web pages out of them to share with the world.

1. Put all the images you want to put on the Photo Web Pages into the same folder. Make sure these are the only images in the folder.

2. Launch Elements and select Automate from the File menu. You don't have to open a file first.

3. Select Web Photo Gallery from the list that appears. The Web Photo Gallery box opens—you can see it here:

4. You can select from three types of pages: Simple, Table, and Vertical Frame. For this practice exercise, choose Table from the drop-down list that appears when you click the down arrow next to the Styles box.

5. Type in the text and choose the settings you want for the Banner; this is the text that will appear at the top of the page.

6. Click the down arrow next to the Options box and select Gallery Images from the list that appears.

7. Give each picture a three-pixel border and set the other options for how the images are sized, as you can see I have done here:

8. Click Source and tell Elements which folder has the images in it that you want to use.

9. Click Destination and tell Elements where to put the finished pages.

10. Elements creates the pages, opening and displaying each image in turn as it works through the process.

When Elements is finished, it will open your browser (the one you see in the Save For Web box) and show you the pages. As you can see from my finished product (see Figure 16-5), the pages are ready to be posted to my Web site.

Use the File | Save As function of your browser to save the Web pages as HTML files. Use Web pages, complete to save the files exactly as you see them in the browser.

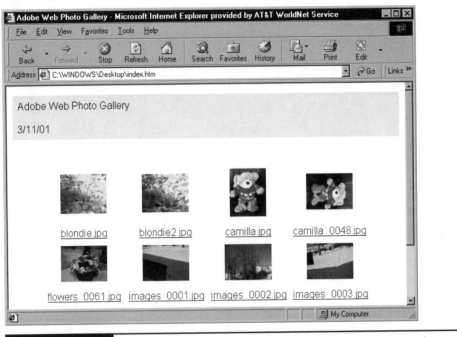

FIGURE 16-5   Elements took my images, made them JPEG images, and arranged them on Web pages for me in just a few seconds

Summary

Well, here we are—at the end of the chapter and the end of the book. What a lot we have gotten done in 16 chapters. I'm happy you stuck with me until the end, and I hope you enjoyed learning how to use Elements. It's a great program full of creative capabilities.

Now that you know how to save your images for the Web, here's a suggestion: Go back through the book, pick some of your favorite projects, save the images as Web graphics, and create your own image portfolio on a Web site.

Even if you've never created a Web site before, it's not that hard to make a simple one, and it's a good next step for you. Chances are if you have an e-mail account your e-mail service provider has set aside some server space for your own personal Web page, and has software on its Web site to help you create a page. Check it out, create your page, and load your images. Then e-mail all your friends to tell them about the page.

16

Index

INTERNATIONAL CONTACT INFORMATION

AUSTRALIA
McGraw-Hill Book Company Australia Pty. Ltd.
TEL +61-2-9417-9899
FAX +61-2-9417-5687
http://www.mcgraw-hill.com.au
books-it_sydney@mcgraw-hill.com

CANADA
McGraw-Hill Ryerson Ltd.
TEL +905-430-5000
FAX +905-430-5020
http://www.mcgrawhill.ca

**GREECE, MIDDLE EAST,
NORTHERN AFRICA**
McGraw-Hill Hellas
TEL +30-1-656-0990-3-4
FAX +30-1-654-5525

MEXICO (Also serving Latin America)
McGraw-Hill Interamericana Editores S.A. de C.V.
TEL +525-117-1583
FAX +525-117-1589
http://www.mcgraw-hill.com.mx
fernando_castellanos@mcgraw-hill.com

SINGAPORE (Serving Asia)
McGraw-Hill Book Company
TEL +65-863-1580
FAX +65-862-3354
http://www.mcgraw-hill.com.sg
mghasia@mcgraw-hill.com

SOUTH AFRICA
McGraw-Hill South Africa
TEL +27-11-622-7512
FAX +27-11-622-9045
robyn_swanepoel@mcgraw-hill.com

**UNITED KINGDOM & EUROPE
(Excluding Southern Europe)**
McGraw-Hill Education Europe
TEL +44-1-628-502500
FAX +44-1-628-770224
http://www.mcgraw-hill.co.uk
computing_neurope@mcgraw-hill.com

ALL OTHER INQUIRIES Contact:
Osborne/McGraw-Hill
TEL +1-510-549-6600
FAX +1-510-883-7600
http://www.osborne.com
omg_international@mcgraw-hill.com